Special Thanks

I would like to thank my lovely wife for her continuing support. Without her, I could not keep working on my passion of helping small business owners navigate the confusing world of financial records.

Secondly, I would like to thank you, the reader of this book. Just as I hope that you gain some much-needed information and understanding, your purchase has helped me greatly in return.

It is to you, aspiring entrepreneur, that I dedicate this book.

Contents

Introduction 12

Chapter 1: Accounting Explained 17

    What is Accounting? 18

    Types of Accounting 19

        Financial Accounting 20

        Managerial Accounting 20

        Cost Accounting 21

    Requirements for Accounting 22

    What is Bookkeeping? 23

    Importance of Bookkeeping 24

    Types of Bookkeeping 25

        Single-entry Bookkeeping 26

        Double-entry System 27

    Comparing Accounting and Bookkeeping 29

    Definition of Accounting Terms 32

        Accounting Equation 33

        Accounting 33

        Accounts Payable 34

        Accounts Receivable 34

        Accrual Accounting 35

        Accruals 35

        Amortization 36

DIY Small Business Accounting

The Easy Way

Learn How to Master GAAP, P&L, Income Statements, Cash Flow, Balance Sheets, Ledgers, Journals & Much More

By

Simon J. Lawrence

Copyright © 2020 – *Lost River Publishing House*

Email: *Publisher@LostRiver.pub*

All Rights Reserved.

No part of this publication may be reproduced, stored in a retrieval system or transmitted in any form or by any means, electronic, mechanical, photocopying, recording or otherwise without the proper written consent of the copyright holder, except as permitted under Sections 107 & 108 of the 1976 United States Copyright Act, without the prior written permission of the publisher.

Lost River Publishing House publishes its books and guides in a variety of electronic and print formats, Some content that appears in print may not be available in electronic format, and vice versa.

Cover design

Lisa Cunningham

First Edition

Asset 36
Audit Trail 36
Auditors 36
Balance Sheet 37
Bookkeeping 37
Budgeting 37
Capital Stock 38
Capital Surplus 38
Capitalized Expense 38
Cash Flow 38
Cash Basis Accounting 39
Chart of Accounts 39
Closing the Books/Year End Closing 40
Cost Accounting 40
Credit 40
Debit 41
Departmental Accounting 41
Depreciation 41
Dividends 41
Double-entry Bookkeeping 42
Equity 42
Financial Accounting 42
Financial Statement 42
Fixed Asset 43
General Ledger 43
Goodwill 43
Income Statement 43
Inventory Valuation 44
Inventory 44

Invoice	44
In the Black	45
In the Red	45
Job Costing	45
Journal	46
Liability	46
Liquid Asset	46
Loan	47
Master Account	47
Net Income	47
Non-cash Expense	47
Non-operating Income	48
Note	48
Operating Income	48
Other Income	49
Payroll	49
Posting	49
Profit	49
Profit/Loss Statement	50
Reconciliation	50
Retained Earnings	50
Revenue	51
Shareholder Equity	51
Single-entry Bookkeeping	51
Statement of Account	52
Subsidiary Accounts	52
Supplies	52
Treasury Stock	53
Write-down/Write-off	53

A Discussion of Stockholder's Equity 53

The Purpose of Accounting 56

    Recording 56

    Planning 57

    Decision Making 57

    Performance 59

    Financial Position 59

    Liquidity 60

    Financing 61

    Control 61

    Accountability 62

    Legal Obligation 63

    Users 63

Chapter 2: Bookkeeping Basics Needed in Accounting 65

Accounting Methods 66

    Cash Method 66

    Accrual Accounting 68

What transactions should be recorded? 70

    Sales and Revenue 70

    Accounts Receivables 71

    Accounts Payable 71

    Summaries of Transactions 72

Understanding Subsidiary Books of Entries 73

The General Journal 74

The General Ledger 78

General Journal vs General Ledger 82

    The Purpose of Use 83

    The Point of Reference 83

    The Length of Use 84

    Recording Style 84

    The Difference in Importance 85

    The Starting Balance 85

    Reporting 86

Trial Balance 87

Chapter 3: Understanding Financial Statements 94

What are financial statements? 95

    Balance Sheet 96

    Income Sheet 97

    Statement of Owner Equity 98

    Cash Flow Statement 99

How to Prepare Financial Statements 99

    Preparing the Balance Sheet 100

    Preparing the (P&L) Profit/Loss Statement 107

    Preparing the Statement of Cash Flow 117

    Preparing the Statement of Retained Earnings 124

How to Interpret Financial Statements 129

    How to Use the Balance Sheet 131

    How to Use the Income Statement 133

    How to Use the Cash Flow Statement 135

    How to Use the Statement of Retained Earnings 137

Chapter 4: Accounting Principles 139

The 4 Principles of Financial Accounting 142
- Cost Principle 142
- Revenue Principle 143
- Matching Principle 144
- Disclosure Principle 145

12 Concepts of GAAP 145
- Accounting Entity 146
- Going Concern 146
- Measurement 147
- Units of Measure 147
- Historical Cost 148
- Materiality 148
- Estimates and Judgments 149
- Consistency 149
- Conservatism 150
- Periodicity 150
- Substance Over Form 151
- Accrual Basis of Presentation 151

What is the accounting equation? 152
- Assets 155
- Liabilities 156
- Shareholders' Equity 157
- Applying the Accounting Equation to Corporations 158
- Applying the Accounting Equation to an LLC 159
- Applying the Accounting Equation in a Partnership 160
- Applying the Accounting Equation to a Sole Proprietorship 161

Chapter 5: Financial Statements Analysis and Analysis Tools ..163

Analysis Tools Used in Accounting 164
- Comparative Statements 166
- Common Size Statements 166
- Trend Analysis 167
- Ratio Analysis 168

Liquidity Ratios 168
- Why liquidity ratios? 169
- Types of Liquidity Ratios 170

Solvency Ratios 172
- Debt to Equity Ratio 173
- Debt Ratio 175
- Proprietary Ratio 176
- Interest Coverage Ratio 177

Profitability Ratios 177
- Margin Ratios 178
- Return Ratios 181

Activity Ratios 183
- Total Assets Turnover Ratio 183
- Fixed Assets Turnover Ratio 184
- Current Assets Turnover Ratio 184
- Working Capital Turnover Ratio 185
- Stock Turnover Ratio 185
- Debtor Turnover Ratio 186
- Creditors' Turnover Ratio 187

Cash Flow Ratios 188
- Current Liability Coverage Ratio 188

Price to Cash Flow Ratio 189

Cash Flow Margin Ratio 190

Cash Flow Coverage Ratio 190

Coverage Ratios 192

Interest Coverage Ratio 192

Debt Service Coverage 192

Asset Coverage Ratio 193

Cash Coverage Ratio 194

Accounting Software 194

Microsoft Excel 196

QuickBooks 200

Square 204

FreshBooks 208

Chapter 6: A Real-world Example Project 213

Step 1: Fish Out Financial Statements 213

Step 2: Transfer Financial Information to Excel Spreadsheets 214

Step 3: Create Analytical Tools 214

Step 4: Create and Answer Managerial Questions 214

Step 5: Find Answers to Your Questions 215

Conclusion 216

Introduction

Statistics show that about 66% of small businesses in the UK are at risk of dissolution due to the mismanagement of accounting paperwork. In the US, about 64% of small businesses spend over $1,000 annually on tax preparation.

If these figures are anything to go by, accounting is one of the most vital sections of any business or company. You can play around with any other department, but you must ensure that your books are in order. Building a successful business starts by developing strategic bookkeeping practices.

Through bookkeeping and accounting, you will be able to track down all your resources and invest wisely. Unfortunately, most businesses do not pay the necessary attention to bookkeeping and accounting; those that do only focus on bookkeeping for tax purposes. Understanding that accounting is designed for your business growth will help you invest more time and effort into the practice.

I have been a practicing accountant for the past 22 years. In my short career, I have seen many businesses collapse due to the mismanagement of accounting paperwork. In my analysis, poor record-keeping and failure to take accounting seriously are the leading contributors to business failure.

Most businesses realize their mistakes when it is already too late. Unfortunately, once the damage is done, you can never find a way back. Keep in mind that even securing a loan depends on having clean accounting records. In other words, poor accounting equates to business suicide. If your accounts do not show consistency and accuracy, chances are that you will fall into trouble with lenders and other partners.

In the past few years, I have dedicated myself to helping small businesses maintain healthy accounting practices. Accounting might be one of the most time-consuming tasks of a business, but it is also the most rewarding. Businesses that have adopted the best accounting practices enjoy the fruits in the long run.

Unfortunately, the fruits of accounting may not be seen in just a few short months. Most business owners only choose to invest in departments that bring instant returns. This is a gross mistake that has led to a lot of cash flow problems for small businesses. The idea of accounting is based on helping your business grow for the long term.

If you are a business manager or an owner of a small business, this book is for you. This book is geared towards helping individuals who have never attended an accounting class but have to manage accounts in their business.

If you do not have any skill in accounting, you should not worry so much about the technical terms used by accountants. You can learn everything you need to know about accounting in just a week. This book will help you learn all the basics of accounting and be able to prepare and interpret your financial statements.

In this book, we will cover the following topics :

- Introduction to accounting and definition of counting terms.

- Introduction to books of accounts and the best practices in bookkeeping.

- Analysis and use of financial statements. We will look at what they are and how they can help your business.

- Accounting analysis tools and how they are beneficial to your business.

- Accounting software and how to use it.

- Real-life examples, illustrations, screenshots, and other practical tools to help you process the content.

These key areas of accounting will help you understand what accounting entails, the principles that guide the practice, and the benefit of the practice. Further, the book will help you understand how to read and interpret your financial statements. The book breaks down the key financial statements into categories based on their use. You will learn the importance of each statement to your business, investors, the tax department, and other interested parties.

If you are a business owner or a manager looking to grow your accounting skills, welcome aboard. This book will help you learn everything you need to know in a simple step by step process.

Chapter 1: Accounting Explained

When most people hear the term accounting, they think about numbers, tables, and charts. These are very scary elements of academia that only a few wish to associate with. Consequently, most people prefer leaving accounting to experts. However, running a business demands that you understand the basics of accounting.

As a matter of fact, you should be savvier than your accountant if you expect to benefit the most from your accountant's office. In this chapter, we are going to define what accounting is and help you understand what it means to be an accountant. You will realize that you do not necessarily have to be a mathematical genius to be an accountant. After all, if you can run or manage a business, you are already an accountant. All you need to do is gain the skills needed to follow the organized accounting principles.

What is Accounting?

Accounting is the process of analyzing, summarizing, and reporting financial transactions. The process of accounting starts by recording and systematically keeping the transactions. Once the records are recorded and filed, they are summarized into meaningful reports and shared with oversight regulators, tax agencies, the board of management, interested investors, and shareholders, among other entities. In the simplest terms, the accountant's work is to prepare a report card on the performance of a business or company.

The financial statements used in accounting are accurate transactions recorded throughout an accounting period. In most cases, the work of recording, verifying, and filing transactions is done by a bookkeeper. Once the financial records have been obtained in an orderly manner, the accountant uses them to prepare financial reports. The financial reports are much easier to interpret and offer valuable information on the status of the business.

In most firms, accounting tasks are handled by an accountant, although in some instances, the work is handled by a bookkeeper. The reports generated by the accountant are handed to the management, which in turn uses them in decision making. The process of accounting is very vital in determining the tax to be paid by the business and ensuring that the taxes are paid.

Types of Accounting

There are three main types of accounting: financial, managerial, and cost accounting.

Financial Accounting

Financial accounting refers to the process used to generate annual and interim financial reports. Financial accounting is the backbone of accounting in all businesses. It is the process that sheds a clear light on the growth of the business and provides indications for the future. The results of financial accounting are usually summarized in financial statements. The most important financial statements are; the balance sheet, income statement, and the statement of cash flow.

In accounting, accuracy is the most important value. At the end of the financial year, accounting summaries are audited by an independent CPA firm. For publicly traded companies, financial audits are compulsory.

Managerial Accounting

Managerial accounting is similar to financial accounting; the only difference is that the information obtained is utilized for the growth of the business. In managerial accounting, the data is further broken down and used to make key investment decisions. A financial accountant sits on the board of management and helps the company make the right decisions by providing valuable information.

Managerial accounting includes many other aspects of accounts. For instance, financial accounting has to cater to budgeting, forecasting, and planning. This is achieved through financial analysis tools that provide a clear picture of the future.

Cost Accounting

Cost accounting refers to a type of accounting that helps the business manage cash flow. In other words, this type of accounting helps a business make the right costing decisions. Without costing accounting, a business may engage in a costly production process and end up making losses.

Essentially, this type of accounting considers the various costs related to producing and selling a product. The information provided by costing accountants is used by analysts, business owners, and managers to make key decisions.

In cost accounting, money is considered to be an economic factor in production, while in financial accounting, money is seen as a measure of the company's performance.

Requirements for Accounting

Generally, most people can account for their finances. However, for any person to be qualified as an accountant, he/she should be in a position to follow certain principles of bookkeeping and accountancy. In most cases, accountants are required to follow the Generally Accepted Accounting Principles (GAAP). GAAPs are a set of rules that are used in bookkeeping and preparation of financial reports in the US. The GAAP rules and principles are based on double-entry accounting. In double-entry accounting, every transaction is recorded as both debit and credit.

In accounting, a business can have so many books of accounts or several accounts in the same ledger. Accounts can be either debit or credits. Any account that has the potential of adding money or assets to the business is a debit account, while accounts that are likely to reduce the assets or finances of the business are debits.

What is Bookkeeping?

Bookkeeping is the practice of recording, reconciling, and storing the financial transactions of a business or company. In bookkeeping, financial transactions are first recorded in subsidiary books of entry before being transferred to the general ledger. We will have a look at ledgers and the books of entry in a short while.

A bookkeeper is mandated with the task of ensuring that all the transactions of a company are recorded and filed. A bookkeeper also has to find the original documents that prove the occurrence of a transaction. Bookkeeping duties include filing of receipts, invoices, and printouts. Such source documents are needed to prove that a transaction has taken place. It is the work of a bookkeeper to ensure that they are stored in an organized manner and secured.

The most important trait for a bookkeeper is accuracy. All the transactions recorded in subsidiary books and the general ledger should be verifiable. In other words, the accounts debited should correspond to the accounts credited. If there are found to be inconsistencies within the credit and debit accounts, the bookkeeper should provide documents that support the anomalies. Accuracy helps reduce fines from the tax agencies. If you are found to be violating bookkeeping principles or providing inaccurate account values, you may be fined for such actions.

Importance of Bookkeeping

Proper keeping of accounting records gives your business a clear indication of its performance. Without proper bookkeeping, you may not be able to assess the growth of your business. It is through the recorded transactions that a business can establish the profit, the cost of production, sources of revenue, and possible expenditure loopholes.

In other words, once you start a business, you must ensure that you have a bookkeeper to help in recording all your transactions. With that said, most small businesses do not hire full-time accountants. Most small companies prefer hiring a bookkeeper and outsourcing accountancy services from accounting firms. If you can keep the subsidiary books of entry yourself, you do not have to hire a bookkeeper. It is possible to manage your books without having an in-house bookkeeper or accountant. However, the work of bookkeeping is labor-intensive. Only opt for maintaining your books personally if you have plenty of time on your hands.

Types of Bookkeeping

Bookkeeping can broadly be categorized into two types: double entry and single entry. In essence, bookkeeping is just recording entries into your books of accounts. These entries can either be recorded using the double-entry format or the single entry format.

Single-entry Bookkeeping

In single-entry bookkeeping, each item gets its entry in accounting records. In other words, every item that is purchased or sold is recorded in the books of accounting individually. This method of accounting works well for small businesses. Since the method is focused on cash received and paid expenses, it can be used to manage the cost of production and even help prepare certain financial statements.

The single entry system only works if the expenses are entered once they are incurred (cash method). As we will see later, the cash method of accounting works well for small businesses that do not have complex transactions. With the single entry approach, the process is as simple as recording sales and expenses once they happen.

The single entry method uses books of subsidiary entries to record each transaction. The bookkeeper may maintain several subsidiary books of entry such as cash sales journal, cash disbursement journal, and product returns journal, etc. At the end of a certain trading period, the records are reconciled and compared with the bank accounts.

With the single entry method of bookkeeping, transaction recording is straight forward. You can record transactions in books manually, or you may use bookkeeping software to record transactions. This system of recording is simple, and business owners can undertake the task of bookkeeping without hiring an accountant.

Date	Particulars	Income	Expenses	Balance
1-Apr	Balance forwarded			1,000.00
5-Apr	Supplies		200.00	800.00
10-Apr	Sales	500.00		1,300.00
15-Apr	Electric bills		600.00	700.00
20-Apr	Sales	1,000.00		1,700.00
30-Apr	Bank fees		50.00	1,650.00
	Balance			1,650.00

Double-entry System

The double entry system is a bit complex and is often used by large businesses and corporations. The double entry works by first recording a transaction as either income or expense (Debit or credit). After recording the transaction, you trace it to the corresponding account. For instance, if you record a transaction that debits your assets, you need to credit your cash accounts.

The double entry system enables you to track up to 5 accounts at ago: Expenses, revenues, equities, and liabilities. You can also use a simple format with debit and credit columns when preparing a double-entry journal. In this way, the entries are made on accounts that are affected by the same transaction. For instance, if you buy company machinery with money from the bank, the machinery account is debited while the cash account is credited. This way, you can track all transactions individually and verify the authenticity of your records in case of a mistake.

Small businesses are not required to use double-entry by law. If you are running a business that generates less than $1 million in revenue, you can use the single or double entry systems. However, any business making more than $5 million in gross sales or $1 million in gross receipts is required to use the double-entry by law. The double entry system is easy to track down and makes the work of financial auditors easier.

Comparing Accounting and Bookkeeping

Most people have a misconception that bookkeeping and accounting are the same things. However, they are slightly different, as you can see from the definitions above. The roles and responsibilities of a bookkeeper are different from those of an accountant, although they complement each other. The main role of a bookkeeper is to record transactions in a generally accepted way in the accounting world.

In other words, the work of a bookkeeper is to record financial transactions following accounting principles. On the other hand, the work of an accountant is to summarize the transactions into actionable financial reports. The accountant can also offer advisory, help in tax processing, and explain certain financial reports to the management.

The roles of a bookkeeper and an accountant meet at the general ledger. A general ledger is a book that summarizes all transaction entries. Bookkeepers can record transactions in subsidiary books of entry and summarize them in the ledger book. This means that the work of a bookkeeper involves day to day tracking of transactions. Once the bookkeeper is done with the ledger book, the accountant takes over. The accountant gets to review the ledger book and verify the content. Once verified, the accountant summarizes the information from the ledger into financial reports and analytical tools.

Here are the main differences between bookkeeping and accounting.

- Bookkeeping is mainly related to identifying, measuring, and recording financial transactions, while accounting refers to summarizing and interpreting financial transactions.

- The management of the business cannot use the information in the ledger to make key financial decisions while accounting is mainly done to provide information that is necessary for making future investment decisions.

- The main objective of bookkeeping is to keep records systematically, while the main objective of accounting is to gauge the financial position of a business.

- In bookkeeping, no financial reports are prepared while in accounting, the main aim is to prepare financial reports.

- Bookkeeping does not require any special skills and can be done by any person who has a basic understanding of bookkeeping software. On the other hand, accounting requires special skills that help in the preparation of financial statements. For anyone to become an accountant, he/she has to be accredited by the CPA board.

- The process of bookkeeping requires little analysis, while the process of accounting requires in-depth analysis. Further, accounting includes advisory to the board of managers for future investments.

- Bookkeepers are required to be accurate and ensure that all the transactions are recorded, the accuracy of a bookkeeper is overseen by an accountant. The accountant inspects the work of a bookkeeper by preparing financial statements.

- All accountants need to back their knowledge with relevant academic credentials such as a degree and must obtain the title of Certified Public Accountant while bookkeepers don't have to show such credentials.

Definition of Accounting Terms

Accounting is a process that includes plenty of technical, analytical terms. In most cases, it is such terms that make people shy away from financial reports. If you are a business manager, you should at least understand the terms that are used in financial reports. Understanding such terms will help you interpret all the reports and make the best decisions. If you do not learn how to interpret your financial reports, you will be paying your accountants for no reason. At the end of the day, your accountant should help you make the best decision for your business and invest wisely. Here are the commonly used accounting terms and what they mean.

Accounting Equation

The accounting equation is the summary of accounting as a practice. The accounting equation states that **Assets = Liabilities + Equity**. We will define each of these terms as we move on and also look into accounting equations in more detail.

Accounting

Accounting is the process of tracking financial records of a business, summarizing them, and reporting them. As we have already seen, this process simply summarizes the ledger entries into actionable financial reports.

Accounts Payable

Accounts payable is an account entry in the general ledger that represents the liabilities of a business. Anything that has to be paid within the trading period under record is entered as an account payable. For example, if you have received raw materials worth $1,000 on credit, you have to record this transaction under accounts payable. This means that you are in debt of $1,000 to be paid within the current trading period.

Accounts Receivable

Accounts receivables are assets of the business and represent money owed to the business. Accounts receivable entries mainly include all the money of the business that is yet to be received. For instance, if you supplied goods worth $100 to a customer on credit, you should record this amount under accounts receivable.

Accrual Accounting

Accrual accounting is a method of bookkeeping where the entries recorded represent transactions that are completed even though cash has not changed hands. In other words, the accrual method records account receivable as assets of the company even though the money is not yet in the hands of the business and accounts payable as liabilities even though the money is yet to be paid out. For example, if you supplied goods worth $1,000 on credit, the accrual method records this amount as an asset, which means that the transaction is completed in theory.

Accruals

Accrual is a process of recognizing revenue and expenses once they happen. See the example above.

Amortization

Amortization is a process of reducing debts through equal payments that include debts.

Asset

Items that are owned by the company, such as machinery, cash, premises, etc. Assets are categorized in current and long-term assets. We will look at asset classification later.

Audit Trail

A process of investigating transactions recorded in the general ledger to the source. If a transaction is recorded in the ledger book but does not seem to make sense, an auditor may seek clarification by looking at source documents.

Auditors

Accountants who examine the financial records of a business to ascertain their accuracy. An auditor may be a representative of tax agencies or might be hired by the company for internal auditing.

Balance Sheet

A financial statement that summarizes the assets and liabilities of a business. The equation for the balance sheet states that **Assets = Liabilities + Owners Equity**. We will look at the meaning of all these words in a short while.

Bookkeeping

The process of recording, filing, and systematically storing financial transactions.

Budgeting

Budgeting is the practice of allocating funds to ensure that there is continuous cash flow for business operations. Budgeting requires an analysis of the current position of the business and prioritizing key functions. Accountants offer valuable information through financial reports that help in budgeting.

Capital Stock

The total amount of preferred and common stock issued by a company. In simple terms, it is the total stock for a traded company.

Capital Surplus

The excess of common shares. Surplus stock is often sold to outside individuals.

Capitalized Expense

Expenses that are accumulated over a long time.

Cash Flow

The net money coming into the business. Cash flow usually represents the difference between money in and money out of the business. Positive cash flow shows that the business is making more money than it spends, while a negative money flow shows the reverse. If cash flow is not accounted for well, a business may experience operational constrains.

Cash Basis Accounting

Cash basis accounting is a method of accounting where transactions are only recognized after money changes hands. It is the opposite of accrual accounting, where expenses are recognized before cash changes hands.

For example, if you are using the cash method, you cannot maintain accounts payable and accounts receivable accounts. The transactions that are recorded are either cash or expenses that are already completed.

Chart of Accounts

A list of accounts used to record financial transactions in an organization. Different organizations used a different number of accounts to record financial transactions. For instance, one business may maintain accounts receivable, while another may only maintain a cash account.

Closing the Books/Year End Closing

Closing the books refers to the final summary of all transactions at the end of the financial year of the business. This allows you to start a new trading period with clean records.

Cost Accounting

A type of accounting that is used to determine the cost of operations. It helps reduce expenses and increase profitability.

Credit

An accounting entry that increases liability for the business. Credit is usually entered on the right hand of the column. Credit entries increase equity, liability, and revenue and decrease assets and expenses.

Debit

Entries recorded on the left column of any account. Assets and expenses increase on the debit side while liabilities decrease.

Departmental Accounting

Analyzing summarizing transactions occurring according to various departments.

This type of accounting helps to determine the most beneficial departments in the business.

Depreciation

The decrease in value of an asset. For instance, a van bought by the company ten years ago should be worth much less at the moment.

Dividends

Profits returns that are shared with shareholders of a company.

Double-entry Bookkeeping

A type of bookkeeping where each transaction is recorded in two accounts (debit and credit).

It helps with the tracking of transactions.

Equity

A representation of the value of ownership. The stake that a person holds in a company can be referred to as his/her equity.

Financial Accounting

Type of accounting that is primarily focused on preparing financial reports for external users.

Financial Statement

A summary document detailing the financial activities of a business over a given timeframe.

Fixed Asset

A property owned by the business that can be used for a long time. In most cases, fixed assets give returns in more than a year.

General Ledger

A book of accounts where summaries of all transactions are recorded as either debit or credit.

Goodwill

An unseen asset that a business enjoys due to its reputation. For instance, if you were to buy a company like Nike, you will have to pay a lot more for the reputation of the brand than the amount you will pay for physical assets.

Income Statement

A financial statement that summarizes the revenue and expenses of a business. The income statement helps us determine profit and loss for a company over a given period.

Inventory Valuation

A method of valuation used in real estate business appraisal.

Inventory

Inventory entails all the materials and products that have already been produced. In the retail business, inventory simply refers to products that are yet to be sold. In production, inventory includes raw material, material in the production process, and goods that have already been produced.

Invoice

A financial document used to show the amount of money owed for goods or services. You can receive an invoice from your supplier for the raw materials ordered.

In the Black

This refers to the occurrence of a profit in the books. This term is the opposite of "in the red." It is also the origin of the "holiday" called "Black Friday" in the United States. This is the Friday after Thanksgiving and is considered the biggest shopping day of the year when retailers expect to be "in the black" due to a high volume of sales, hence the term.

In the Red

Refers to a loss in the books of accounts. It is the opposite of "in the black" above. The two statements originated during the days of paper bookkeeping. When the bookkeeper recorded a ledger entry in black, it meant that a profit had been made, and when an entry was recorded in red, it meant that a loss had been made.

Job Costing

Refers to calculations made to determine the cost of a certain job against the revenue it generates.

Journal

The first book where a transaction is recorded. Transactions are recorded in the order of their occurrence.

Liability

Liabilities refer to what the business owes other businesses or individuals. For instance, if the business has to pay a longer-term loan, the loan can be classified as a long term liability. On the other hand, if a business is supposed to pay employees, the salaries payable can be classified as short term liabilities.

Liquid Asset

Refers to cash or assets that can be converted into cash in less than a year.

In other words, an asset that is likely to be turned into cash in months can be referred to as an asset.

Loan

Money borrowed from a financial lender or an individual. Loans are usually paid back over a long period with interest.

Master Account

A master account is an account that has subsidiary accounts. For instance, the cash account can be termed as the master account if it has other smaller accounts inside. Under the cash account, you could have a cash sales account, individual asset accounts, etc.

Net Income

This refers to the total revenue minus expenses, taxes, and depreciation. It is the value that represents the overall earnings of the business within the said trading period.

Non-cash Expense

A non-cash expense does not require money being given out. An excellent example of a non-cash expense is depreciation.

Non-operating Income

Income that is not generated from day to day operations of a business. For instance, if you sell a long term asset such as the van of a company, the revenue received is classified as non operating income.

Note

A document that gives an assurance or a promise that a debt owed will be paid. Sometimes referred to as a "promissory note."

Operating Income

The net operating income refers to the amount earned from daily business operations. It is calculated by subtracting expenses from revenue.

Other Income

Income that cannot be classified as operation or non-operating. For example, non-recurring income is earned as a result of loans given out. If you give a loan out, you will receive interest on the money given out.

Payroll

An account that lists all the employees of the company and their salaries.

Posting

Posting is technically used to mean recording ledger entries.

Profit

Profit refers to the amount a business generates above the expenses. To determine your profit, subtract taxes and interest from total revenue.

Profit/Loss Statement

A financial document that discloses the earning of a business. The profit and loss statement compares the revenue and expenditure to determine the net profit. It is sometimes referred to as a "P&L Statement."

Reconciliation

The act of proving account balances as indicated in the general ledger.

For instance, if the general ledger shows that $1,000 was withdrawn from the bank account on May 31st, you can reconcile by ensuring that the bank balances at that date are as indicated in the books.

Retained Earnings

Also referred to as surplus profit. This refers to money that is left after paying all the bills, and shareholders dividend has been distributed.

Revenue

The total amount of money that comes into a business during a given operating period.

Also known as gross income.

Shareholder Equity

Owners' equity refers to the part of the business that is owned by you.

If you start a business, the capital you invest in your equity at the beginning of the business.

Owners' equity grows or reduces depending on the value of retained earnings over time.

Single-entry Bookkeeping

Method of bookkeeping where one entry is made per transaction. It is the opposite of double-entry and does not include the debit and credit format.

Statement of Account

A written statement that summarizes all charges and payments. For instance, the statement may contain accounts receivable and accounts receivable statements.

Subsidiary Accounts

Subsidiary accounts refer to accounts of original entry. They are usually under a control account in the general ledger. For instance, accounts such as office supplies, or cleaning supplies may all be classified under the supplies account.

Supplies

Materials and tools needed for day to day operations of a business. They are usually consumable materials and are not classified under inventory. For instance, cleaning supplies are necessary for general hygiene but cannot be classified as raw materials or stock for the production process.

Treasury Stock

Shares that a company retains of buses back from the public.

Write-down/Write-off

An accounting entry that reduces the value of an asset. A write off asset might be deemed valueless to the company and may be given away for free or disposed of.

A Discussion of Stockholder's Equity

Stockholder's equity refers to the portion of the business that you own. In terms of a corporation, it relates to the portion of the company that common stockholders own.

It is also called "shareholder's equity." This amount is reported in a section of the company's balance sheet for a given reporting period.

When creating a balance sheet, the sum of the entries on the right side must balance with the sum of entries on the left side. Here is the formula used to create a balance sheet.

Assets = Liabilities + Owners equity

Owners' equity in this equation represents the value of assets above liabilities. In other words., if the assets have appreciated over the course of running the business, the owner of the business lays a claim to this appreciation.

The owner's equity is calculated cumulatively. To determine the owner's equity in the current financial years, you need to add the current retained earnings to the owner's equity at the start of the financial year.

Let's look at an example to help you understand what the owner's equity really is. Let's say you choose to start a business by investing $30,000 worth of capital. Assuming that this capital is your money and is not borrowed in the business name, your business will be worth $ 30,000 in assets and $0 in liabilities.

However, if you start buying assets and realize that the $30,000 is not enough to purchase all the assets you need to run your business, you may be forced to borrow some money. Let's say you decide to borrow $5,000 to purchase your current business premise. At this stage, your total business assets will be $35,000, but your equity will be $30,000.

Assuming that the business starts operating and makes a profit for 43 consecutive years. You pay off your loan at the rate of $1,000 per year, and you end up paying about $3,000 in 3 years. At this time, your owner's equity will have grown from $30,000 to $33,000. This is because the liabilities of the business have reduced, and the assets have increased.

This is a simple explanation of what the owner's equity is. In big businesses and corporations, calculating the owner's equity might be a bit complex. You should first calculate your retained earnings to determine the owner's equity.

The Purpose of Accounting

You may ask, why exactly do we have to keep records and prepare accounts? Well, if you love your business, this is a question you should never ask. As I mentioned in my introduction, most people engage in accounting for the wrong purposes. Although filing taxes is an integral part of accounting, it is not the only reason you have to keep records. Here are the key objects for accounting.

Recording

The first objective for accounting is to keep records. It is paramount to ensure that you maintain systematic, complete, and accurate records of all your transactions. Having orderly records will make it easy for you to review your transactions at any given time. The records should also serve as proof of your income and expenses in case anyone wants to see it. Systematic record keeping forms the backbone of accounting.

Planning

The other important objective of accounting is planning. Through accounting, we get to determine the financial strength of the business. After determining the financial strength, we can make critical decisions that affect operations, labor force, and strategic investments.

The best way to plan is by using a budget. Many forms of budgeting can be applied in planning, as we will see later. Budgets are necessary to help you prepare by anticipating future business needs. An accountant should help the board of managers determine the business's anticipated future needs for easy planning and budgeting.

Decision Making

The objective of accounting is to help a business make the right decisions. Through the data obtained and trajectories observed, managers can create policies that ensure efficiency in the running of the company. Some of the decisions that can be arrived at through accounting include:

- The price to be charged on products and services in order to meet production costs.

- Products that should be prioritized in case of a shortage in cash.

- The financial needs of the business- whether the business needs to acquire financing.

- To determine the viability of business opportunities. Determines whether a company should invest in specific business opportunities.

- Determines the products that the company should continue offering, depending on their performance and production costs.

- Helps determine the suitability of an individual or a business for credit.

Performance

The other objective of accounting is to determine the performance of the business. You can determine how well the business is performing by summarizing the available financial information. Over the years, you get to see whether your business is growing, declining, or stagnant. A company must have tools that measure performance from the start. This way, they can compare performance over the years to determine growth.

Financial Position

The other important objective of accounting is to determine the financial position of a business or organization. The financial position of business mainly displays the financial strength of a business at a particular time. Through accounting, you can determine:

- The cumulative capital invested in the business.

- How much money is utilized by the business to run daily operations?

- Accumulate income of the business over its lifespan.

- Cumulative debts and liabilities.

- The amount of cash available in your assets.

Liquidity

The other important objective of accounting is to determine the liquidity of a business. As mentioned in the introduction, most small businesses fail due to mismanagement of funds.

Accounting helps us determine the amount of cash and liquid assets available for the business to utilize. Having such information is very important to help maintain cash flow. Without a proper understanding of your liquidity, you may run into problems with cash flow.

Financing

Accounting provides the needed information and records to help secure funding. Although most people only engage in accounting for the IRS, you actually need proper records to secure a loan. Whether you apply for a bank loan or an investment from shareholders, you must have the necessary accounting documents. You are required to provide the history of your transactions in the past 5 years or so. In most cases, the financier will have auditors go through your documents to prove their authenticity.

Control

The other key objective of accounting is to put in place control measures. As a business manager, you need to put internal control measures that determine cash flow in place. If you allow all employees to handle cash, complete transactions, and authorized payments, you will be giving room for fraud. Through accounting, you can determine vulnerable departments and put in place measures. For instance, you may formulate a policy that requires transactions above a specific limit about to go through the manager's office. This way, you reduce the chances of fraud at lower levels.

Accountability

It is impossible to operate a publicly-traded company without accountability. Accountability means that every person is held responsible for their actions. For instance, the board of management should be accountable to the shareholders. The shareholders should get the right information when they need it and should have access to their money when it is time.

In the same way, accounting encourages accountability within the business. The management can hold the accounting office accountable for any errors in transactions. Accounting can help track transactions down to specific individuals who may be involved in fraud.

Legal Obligation

The other objective of accounting is to fulfill the legal requirement.

This is probably the reason why most businesses invest in bookkeeping and accounting. The law requires all businesses to maintain accurate records of their transactions. Further, publicly traded companies are required to report their financial statements to the shareholders and tax authorities.

Accounting is also key since it helps organizations determine their financial rights and obligations. If you do not record your transactions well, you may end up paying excess taxes and being denied your rights. With proper records, you can fight against injustice and prove the recorded transactions in your books.

Users

Final Accounting also has the objective of notifying investors about the progress of your business. Financial statements can be used by employees, the press, investors, and other entities that may be interested. Since accounting fulfills the information needs of diverse stakeholders, it is in your best interest to invest in the right accounting practices.

Chapter 2: Bookkeeping Basics Needed in Accounting

As we have already seen, bookkeeping and accounting are closely related. As a matter of fact, bookkeeping is a minor part of accounting. It Is crucial that an accountant should be able to manage bookkeeping tasks. In most small businesses, the accountant is mandated with bookkeeping and accounting tasks.

Most small businesses do not have a budget to hire a bookkeeper and an accountant at the same time. For this reason, an accountant should be able to record transactions in the most orderly way. So, what are the basic bookkeeping skills that are needed in accounting?

Accounting Methods

Accounting methods refer to the standard way of recording transactions. Although accounting standards are set for accountants, the work of recording transactions is mainly handled by bookkeepers. Any person who identifies as a bookkeeper should be aware of the available accounting methods and should adhere to them.

Generally, there are 2 accounting methods used in bookkeeping: cash and accrual methods.

Cash Method

The cash method is commonly used by small businesses. In this method, transactions are only recognized once money changes hands. In other words, a transaction cannot be recorded down before the money has been handed over. This principle works both ways for payments and revenue. If you are to pay your employees at the end of the month, you cannot record that transaction until the money has been transferred to employees. In the same way, if you sell goods on credit, you cannot record that amount until the goods have been paid for.

The cash method, therefore, does not have accounts payable and accounts receivables. This means that the process of accounting only caters to what the business has received and spent.

This method works well for small businesses that do not have complex transactions. If you are running a small retail business of a company, you may choose to use the cash method. The benefit of this method is that it does not account for money that is yet to be paid. Consequently, you may never be taxed for money that is not in your bank account. For instance, if you supply goods worth $3,000 on December 31st, you do not have to include this amount in your accounts, unless the money is paid on that date.

Cash accounting is much simple and straightforward. It is simple to handle and determine cash flow. If you are new to accounting and want to manage your cash quickly, you can start with a cash accounting method.

Accrual Accounting

The other accounting method that is commonly used is accrual accounting. Accrual accounting works well for established businesses and large corporations. Unlike the cash method, the accrual method recognizes transactions as they happen and not when money is exchanged. In other words, this method s based on trust between trade partners. As long as goods have been supplied, the company has to record that the transaction took place even before receiving payment.

This method is beneficial in several ways. First, it makes the work of managing complex accounts easier. With complex business, it is not easy to track down transactions by using the cash method. Although small businesses prefer using the cash method, some prefer using accrual. While there is nothing wrong with the accrual method, it may not work out better for a small business.

In most cases, the accrual method does not cater to the actual account balance. It only helps show the amount of money that the business is generating. If you have limited finances, using such a method may lead to cash flow problems. On the other hand, if you are running a large business, you accept the full value of your business by using the cash business.

The other benefit of the accrual method is that it helps plan for the future. It provides the necessary data required to plan ahead. Unfortunately, you may end up paying taxes for money you have not received. For instance, if you are supposed to receive cash in January for goods that were supplied in December, you have to pay taxes for such goods. This might affect your business if the pending transaction has significant financial implications for your business.

What transactions should be recorded?

In accounting, the way you record your transactions is very important. The types of accounts you wish to maintain depend on the accounting method you use. The common transactions that are recorded include:

Sales and Revenue

You must have records that show your sales and revenue. These are the primary entries that help in tracking the finances of a business. The sales transactions should be recorded independently in a sales journal. This helps differentiate between cash sales and sales on credit. You may choose to have different sales accounts in the sales journal. For instance, most people divide the sales journal into a purchase account, Cash receipts, and sales returns. You can further break down your account, depending on the type of business that you run.

Besides the sales journal, you also have to create a unique account for other sources of revenue. For instance, if your company offers services instead of products, you could name your account according to the services provided.

Accounts Receivables

Accounts receivable is an account that is used to record all the revenue of the company that is yet to be received. Running accounts receivable helps in tracking debts and following up on payments. Although those who use the cash method do not keep accounts receivable accounts, it is recommended to have one. It is paramount to manage accounts receivable, especially if you give out products on credit or you lend out cash. This way, you can easily track all the finances of the organization that are due to be paid.

Accounts Payable

Accounts payable is the opposite of accounts receivable. Accounts payable record down all the transactions that are complete, but you are yet to release the funds. For instance, if you purchase raw material on credit, you have to record the transaction under accounts payable. As it is the case with accounts receivable, most people who operate accounts payable use the accrual method. However, even if you use the cash method, it is recommended that you run accounts payable for personal use. This helps you track down your debts. Without the accounts payable, you may end up making a loss or run into cashflow problems. Accounts payable also help track down the performance of the business. You can look at your pending bills and determine which ones to prioritize to avoid running into cash flow problems.

Summaries of Transactions

Finally, you need to record summaries of transactions. As we have seen, the key transactions to record include the sales and expenses of the business. After recording all the important transactions, you have to record a summary. Individual transactions are recorded in journals. For instance, you could record the transactions in the sales journal to represent all types of activities in the sales department. After recording in the sales journal, sum up the transactions, and transfer them to the sales account in the general ledger.

Transaction summaries are often written in the general ledger. After recording all individual transactions in the respective books of original entry, you sum them up and transfer to the general ledger. With that said, it is necessary to ensure that all your transactions in the journals add up. If you transfer erroneous transactions to the general ledger, you will have a hard time trying to prove that all the transactions took place.

Understanding Subsidiary Books of Entries

Every accountant must have the knowledge and skills of a bookkeeper. This means that accounting itself starts with bookkeeping. Even though the accountant is not responsible for recording transactions, he/she should be able to interpret the available entries. In the same way, you cannot manage a business unless you can interpret the records. You should be able to read and understand subsidiary books of entry so that you can prove the authenticity of financial statements.

Most business owners and managers make the mistake of relying on the information provided by accountants. If you do not go the extra mile of providing the information, you may end up losing huge sums of money. Most accountants gauge your understanding of accounting terms when they start working for your company. If they realize that you are clueless, they find ways to take advantage.

The General Journal

A general journal is a book of original entries in which all entries that do not fall under specialty journals are entered. A specialty journal is a journal that records all original entries in a specific department. There are four main specialty journals: sales journal, cash receipts journal, a purchases journal, and a cash disbursement journal. Each of these journals are books of original entry and record transactions happening in respective accounts. However, there are some transactions that cannot be classified as either sales, cash, purchases, or cash disbursements. It is such transactions that are recorded in the general journal.

A company may have more than four specialty journals, depending on its needs. Companies that have many processes tend to have more transactions. In such a case, the company may have several specialty journals.

All other transactions that cannot fall under the available specialty journals are entered in the general journal. Transactions that are commonly entered in the specialty journal include:

- Accounts receivable
- Accounts payable
- Equipment
- Accumulated depreciation
- Expenses
- Interest income

As we have already seen, there are two methods of bookkeeping. You can either use the double-entry or single entry method of bookkeeping. With the general journal, double-entry is the commonly used approach. This way, it is much easy to track down transactions. Since a general journal is often used by many complex businesses, every transaction is recorded under two accounts. This way, it is much simple to determine the accounts affected and keep source documents.

The general rule of bookkeeping is the assumption that there are two equal and opposite accounts for all transactions. In other words, if one account is debited, there must be another account that is credited with the same amount.

For example, if your company purchases inventory worth of $5,000 using cash, the cash account has to be credited, and the inventory account debited by the same amount. This means that the general journal can experience two entries or one entry with the other entry being registered in a specialty journal.

For example, if your general journal lists account receivable and inventory accounts, one transaction can affect all the accounts. Say you have supplied goods worth $5,000 to a client, and you want to receive inventory worth the same amount from the same client. You can decide to receive your goods and debit the accounts receivable while crediting the inventory accounts. In this way, the two accounts affected are under the general journal. However, in the case where cash is used to pay for the inventory directly, the accounts affected are inventory account under the general ledger and the cash account, which is a specialty journal.

The general journal is just a table made up of rows and columns. It may consist of 4 to 5 columns, depending on your organization. The main entries include:

- The date of the transaction
- Short description/memo
- The debit amount
- Credit amount
- A reference number

Date	Account Title and Description	Debit	Credit	Reference
31/7/2018	Depreciation Expense	20000		A2018-614
	- Accumulated Depreciation		20000	
	To record depreciation for July 2018			
1/8/2018	Inventory	5000		A2018-544
	- Cash		5000	
	To record inventory purchase			
2/8/2018	Utilities	1000		A2018-125
	- Cash		1000	
	To record August 2018 utilities purchase			
3/8/2018	Cash	15000		A2018-687
	- Sales		15000	
	Collected the cash for sales to be recorded in sales account			
4/8/2018	Cash	75000		A2018-619
	- Capital		75000	
	Owner contributed capital to the business			

In the example above, you can see that each transaction is recorded under two lines. The lines help us distinguish the credit from debit accounts.

The General Ledger

A general ledger represents a record-keeping system for a business or company. The main entries in a general ledger are summaries of transactions as recorded in the general journal. The transactions are recorded either as debit or credit, and all the entries can be validated by preparing a trial balance. The general ledger is opened from the start of the business and keeps all the records of business transactions throughout its history.

The general ledger is an important part of accounting because it holds all the information needed to prepare financial statements. The transactions in a general ledger are divided into assets, liabilities, and owners' equity. Any transaction that reduces the company's assets is seed as a liability. Any transaction that increases a company's worth is recorded as an asset. Other accounts under the general ledger include owners' equity, revenues, and expenses, see the table below.

Debits	Credits
Assets	Liabilities
Expenses	Gains
Losses	Income
Dividends	Revenues
	Equity

The work of creating a general ledger starts by preparing subsidiary books of entry. You need to record individual transactions in the general journals first, sum them up, and transfer the figures to your general ledger. The information is then used to create financial statements such as the balance sheet, profit, and loss statement, cash flow statement, etc.

The first document prepared once all the general ledger data is entered as a trial balance. This is an accounting document that is used to determine the accuracy of the general ledger. If the trial balance does not balance out, the accountant has to trace individual accounts and try to find out the missing transactions.

A general ledger is mostly employed by a business that subscribes to the double-entry method of accounting. This means that each transaction affects at least two sub-ledger accounts. Further, each entry has at least one debit and credit entry. Double-entry transactions in journals are posted in two columns, as we have seen above. The debit entries are posted on the left with the credit entries on the right. The trial balance prepared requires that debit and credit entries must balance. The assumption is that all items within the company are purchased by the capital invested and any money borrowed.

Therefore, the balance sheet must prove that all the assets of the company equal the liabilities and owners' equity.

Assets = Liabilities + Owners equity

The balance sheet is prepared following the above format. The main reason for preparing a trial balance is to determine whether the transactions recorded within a given trading period are accurate. Once the accuracy is determined, the information is used to prepare other financial tools, starting with the balance sheet.

The transaction details available in the general ledger are compiled and summarized at various levels to produce a trial balance. After the trial balance is prepared, the other financial statements are prepared accordingly.

The ledger is also important for monitoring expenses. If your expenses spike over a given period, you can try determining the cause of the spike. Consequently, you can use this information to determine the cost of products. Even though the general ledger may give you pointers on what to do and where to invest, it is not the final statement. Once you compile the full financial statements, you are able to get more detailed data about the performance of your business.

If there are any problems with the general ledger, you need to review all your journals. This can be a hard task, but it helps ensure accountability. Most business managers and owners only focus on reviewing the general ledger and forgo the journals. Your understanding of your general ledger requires that you have a look at the general journal and specialty journals. All the specialty journals should have transactions indicated by date and the accounts affected. Such information is valuable when reviewing your final financial statements too.

General Journal vs General Ledger

The role played by the general journal, and the general ledger may be different, but they are all very important to the business. It is impossible to prepare general ledger without having a general journal and specialty journals. Further, it is impossible to prepare financial reports without having a general ledger. In other words, the journey to preparing effective financial statements starts when you prepare your journals.

There are some key differences between the general journal and the general ledger:

The Purpose of Use

The general journal is only required as a book of original entry. All the entries in the general journal are compiled and transferred to the general ledger. On the other hand, the general ledger acts as the main summary of all transactions in a business. The summary document is vital in preparing financial statements.

The Point of Reference

The other major difference between the two documents is that the general journal acts as a point of reference. If problems arise from the general ledger, the general journal can be reviewed to determine the accuracy of entries. The same cannot be said about the general journal. It is the book of original entry, and any errors found in the general journal can only be traced by looking at source documents such as receipts, invoices, etc.

The Length of Use

The general journal is only used over a given trading period. For instance, the cash sales journal is only relevant to your business during the trading period in which it is recorded. On the other hand, the general ledger is important to the business throughout its life. A general ledger records all transaction summaries from the day you establish your business. It is the document that you will hand over to tax authorities in case an audit is required of your business.

Recording Style

The general journal simply lists specific items or transactions. On the other hand, the general journal only lists transaction summaries. The general journal has to mention the item and also give notes to indicate why it was bought or sold. The general ledger does not provide room for such entries. The only entries that are recorded are the summaries from the general journal and other journals.

The Difference in Importance

The general ledger is of more importance to an institution than the general journal. However, this statement does not mean that the general journal does not offer value to the business. When we track transactions to the books of original entries, we must also look at the general journal. As a document of reference, it must always be available, and all transactions must be recorded accurately.

The Starting Balance

The general ledger starts with an opening balance that is carried forward from the previous trading period. You cannot prepare the general ledger if you do not have the figure carried forward from the previous trading period. On the other hand, a general journal does not have reference to amounts from the preceding trading periods. The journal only records transactions as they happen and indicates which accounts they affect.

Reporting

The general ledger serves as a reporting document since it shows revenue and cost of operations in real-time. Every time you look at the general ledger, you can determine the gross revenue and gross expenditure. This way, you can control the finances of the organization. On the contrary, the general journal cannot be interpreted further than by looking at the figures. The only role the general journal plays is to help store accurate records of the general transactions of a business.

With all that said, both the general ledger and the general journal must be taken seriously. Most people only maintain books of specific entries and forego the general journal. This is a mistake that often leads to unforeseen expenses. When you run the general journal, you can determine the expenses that are not categorized under specific journals.

For instance, if you have debts that you are yet to pay, you may not record them well unless you run a general journal. If debts are left to pile up untraced, you may end up making losses while you think that the business is performing well. To ensure that you maintain a steady flow of finances, try as much as possible to keep a general journal.

When it comes to the general ledger, there are no questions. You must ensure that your general ledger is running and constantly updated. Ensure that all the transactions recorded are accurate and that any missing transactions are tracked down. Most importantly, prepare the trial balance to ensure that the ledger balances out.

Trial Balance

After preparing your general ledger, you need to prove that it is authentic. The only way to prove its authenticity is by preparing a trial balance. The trial balance is the first document prepared before preparing the other financial statements. Although most accountants are in charge of preparing the trial balance, a bookkeeper should also be able to prepare one.

The trial balance is based on the concept that the credit and debit transactions should balance. At the end of the trading period, the credit and debit closing balances are compared by preparing a trial balance.

The trial balance follows a simple format, where items are arranged into debits and credits. On the debit side, you list all the assets and expenses of business while on the credit side, you list all the liabilities, capital, and income.

The main assumption is that all the assets and expenses of a business area s a result of the invested capital, borrowed money (liabilities), or money earned by the business (income) For this reason, all the credit and debit figures of a business should balance.

To prepare a trial balance, you need to get the data from the general ledger. The ledger balances are segregated into credit and debit. You need to evaluate your ledger entries to determine the assets, liabilities, capital, expenses, and income. This way, you are able to format your trial balance and get the total sum at the end of the trading period.

If all your ledger entries are right, the total of debits and credits should balance. This helps you prove that your bookkeeping is okay. If you realize that the balances do not add up, you have to go back to your specialty and general journals to determine the cause of the error. You also have to confirm the balances with the source documents to eliminate all doubts.

A trial balance is not identified as a key financial statement. However, it is just as important as the balance sheet and other financial statements. Some of the purposes of a trial balance include:

- To provide the background information needed for the preparation of financial statements. It is necessary to ensure that general ledger entries are balanced before you start preparing financial statements. Otherwise, you may end up spending too much time on preparing financial statements without accuracy.

- The trial balance ensures that the double-entry system is followed accurately. For every entry that is credited, a corresponding debit is made. The only way to prove that each credit transaction has an equal and opposite transaction is to prepare a trial balance. The trial balance sums up the debit transactions and compares them to the sum of credit transactions.

- The trial balance bridges the gap between financial statements and general ledger. The accuracy of financial statements depends on the accuracy of the general ledger. It is the trial balance that ensures the general ledger is accurately entered. If there are errors in the general ledger, they should be detected at the trial balance level.

- It assists in identifying and correcting all entry errors. The errors that might have been caused by entering a transaction in the wrong account can easily be identified.

<table>
<tr><th colspan="3">ABC LTD
Trial Balance as at 31 December 2011</th></tr>
<tr><th>Account Title</th><th>Debit
$</th><th>Credit
$</th></tr>
<tr><td>Share Capital</td><td></td><td>15,000</td></tr>
<tr><td>Furniture & Fixture</td><td>5,000</td><td></td></tr>
<tr><td>Building</td><td>10,000</td><td></td></tr>
<tr><td>Creditor</td><td></td><td>5,000</td></tr>
<tr><td>Debtors</td><td>3,000</td><td></td></tr>
<tr><td>Cash</td><td>2,000</td><td></td></tr>
<tr><td>Sales</td><td></td><td>10,000</td></tr>
<tr><td>Cost of sales</td><td>8,000</td><td></td></tr>
<tr><td>General and Administration Expense</td><td>2,000</td><td></td></tr>
<tr><td>Total</td><td>30,000</td><td>30,000</td></tr>
</table>

In the example provided above, the title shows the name of the business/ organization and the accounting period.

The accounting period is usually denoted by the ending date, for instance, if you report quarterly, the trial balance should be named according to the final date of the trading period. The account title shows the name of the account from which the balances have been extracted.

Balances that are related to assets and expenses are posted on the left, while balances that are related to liabilities, income, and equity are posted to the right (credit). The sums of the debit and credit figures are shown at the bottom. As you can see from the trial balance, the debit and credit transactions balance to $30,000.

Although the trial balance is one of the important documents, it is not bulletproof. This document can help you detect some errors in your general ledger, but it also has plenty of limitations. Some of the limitations include:

- The trial balance cannot give proof that a transaction was not recorded. This is a big problem considering that there are cases where transactions are completely omitted from books.

- The trial balance might also balance despite having a wrong entry on both the credit and debit side. For instance, if you bought furniture at $4,000 and you recorded that the furniture was bought at $400. The trial balance might still balance as long as the transactions reflect in credit and debit sides.

The only way to ensure that these shortcomings of the trial balance are not experienced is to ensure that all the records of original transactions are recorded simultaneously.

Chapter 3: Understanding Financial Statements

The main work of an accountant is to prepare and interpret financial statements. Such statements are vital in helping determine the expenses of a business, the gross income, and the net income. Further, financial statements help the board of management in making key investment decisions. They are used to predict the future of business, manage cash flow, and determine prospective investments.

What are financial statements?

Financial statements are summaries of all transactions, assets, and liabilities of a company or an organization. Financial statements are prepared as reports to represent the performance of the business at a given point in time. Generally, the commonly used financial statements include the balance sheet, Income sheet, statement of owners' equity, and statement of cash flow.

These financial statements are prepared for varied reasons. First, they act as an indicator that the management uses in making future decisions. They are also used to give the outside world more information about a business. There are many parties outside the business that may be interested in knowing about your financial performance. Some of the individuals who use financial statements include investors, creditors, tax agencies, shareholders, etc. Publicly traded companies are required by law to present the financial statements promptly to tax authorities, shareholders, and any party interested.

Since financial statements are the main source of financial information, they are very important to a business. Financial accounting and reporting places so much emphasis on the accuracy of the figures. Altering figures or reporting financial information that does not match the source documents can lead to legal problems.

Balance Sheet

The balance sheet is a summary of a company's position at a certain point in time. A balance sheet is prepared at the end of a certain trading period. For instance, you may choose to prepare yours quarterly, twice a year, or once a year.

The balance sheet mainly represents the company's assets, liabilities, and owners' equity on the date it is prepared. You should remember that most businesses have liquid assets that are actively trading. The figures given on a balance sheet are only valid for a given period of time and can change within a short time.

With that said, those who look at a balance sheet have less interest in liquid assets. Since a balance sheet compiles all assets and liabilities, it gives the true picture of a company's net worth. It provides clear information on the ability of the company to remain running for the future.

Those who use the balance sheet, such as investors and creditors, can use the information it presents to determine how a company funds its capital assets. Further, the balance sheet shows the strength of the company in terms of its performance, owners' equity, and retained earnings over the years.

Income Sheet

The income sheet is the other important financial statement that is crucial to the company and the outside world. The income statement is a document that shows the revenue and expenses of a company. Most businesses produce an income sheet alongside the balance sheet. Some only produce the income sheet annually, while others produce quarterly or semi-annually. The income sheet is most helpful to the company for internal use. For instance, the board of management can determine which expenses are costing the business the most. After making such determinations, actions that control expenditures are taken.

The income statement can also be used by the outside world. It is most crucial to shareholders and stock traders for publicly traded companies.

The profitability of a company determines its strength in the stock markets and also determines the dividends that shareholders receive.

Statement of Owner Equity

The statement of owners' equity is a document that summarizes the owners worth in the entire business or company.

This statement summarizes the stake of the company that can be referred to as ownership of the common stockholders.

Cash Flow Statement

Lastly, the cash flow statement is a document that shows the flow of funds within a business or organization. The cash flow statement is very important, especially for internal business uses. With the cash flow statement, we can determine the current financial position of the company. This statement simply summarizes all the sources of revenue and compares them against expenses. This way, you are able to determine the profitability of each process.

How to Prepare Financial Statements

The primary work of an accountant is to prepare financial statements and present them as reports to the management. The accountant should provide the necessary advice to ensure that all the financial instruments are used accordingly. Here is a step by step guide on how to prepare each of the above financial statements.

Preparing the Balance Sheet

Step1: Choose a reporting date and include it in your headline.

The balance sheet is a document that summarizes a company's net worth by comparing assets, liabilities, and owners' equity at a specific time. The assets, liabilities, and owners' equity are not constant. They can change at any time as long as the business is operational. For this reason, you must choose a date that suits your balance sheet.

Different businesses have varied approaches to the time when a balance sheet should be prepared. Most large businesses prepare their balance sheets at the end of the physical year.

However, you are free to choose a date that works for your business. If you are running a small business, I will recommend preparing your balance sheet after 6 months.

Step 2: Distinguish your balance sheet entries.

A balance sheet is made up of three main sections. As we have seen in the balance sheet equation

Assets =Liabilities + Owners equity

For you to be able to prepare your balance sheet, you need to assemble all your assets, liabilities, and determine owners' equity. Thankfully, all these entries can be determined from your ledger books. From your general ledger, pick out all items that represent assets and arrange them on the left-hand side of your balance sheet.

When determining your assets, you should consider the fact that we have current and long-term assets. Current assets represent resources of the business that can be turned into cash in less than a year.

Examples of current assets:

- Short term securities
- Cash at hand and bank
- Accounts receivable

- Stock

You should also consider the long term assets (fixed assets). These are the assets that cannot be converted into cash in a year. Most long term assets are meant to generate income in the long run. Such assets are vital for the continuous operation of the business.

Examples of fixed assets:

- Long term securities
- Goodwill
- Machinery
- Real estate

Listing all assets is never easy, especially in cases where your accounting books are not updated. To ensure that you account for all your current assets, ensure that you consider your inventory, cash at hand and in the bank, accounts receivable, etc. If you miss any of these items, you may end up getting false figures. It is necessary to use the right data so that you can reflect on the real growth of the business over the given trading period.

After identifying your assets, look at your liabilities. Just like it is the case with assets, liabilities are also classified into current and long-term. Liabilities can easily be tracked down within your books of accounts. The ledger book will help you identify any long-term liabilities carried forward from the previous trading periods. To ensure that you have a comprehensive list of all your liabilities, start by listing your current liabilities.

Examples of current liabilities:

- Accounts payable
- Deferred revenue
- Commercial paper

After listing your current liabilities, also list all your long-term liabilities. Long-term liabilities mainly include those that should be repaid in a period exceeding one year. In other words, long term liabilities may include long-term loans or such items. These may be paid over a period of many years.

Examples of long-term liabilities:

- Long-term deferred revenue
- Long-term loan

Step 3: Calculate the owner's equity.

Once you are done with compiling your assets and liabilities, determine the owners' equity. For the reason of determining owners' equity, you should first determine retained earnings.

Owners' Equity = Owners Equity carried Forward + Retained earnings

The equation above helps us determine owners' equity. As you can see from the equation, we cannot determine owners' equity before determining retained earnings. Since owners' equity is part of our balance sheet, it is necessary to first prepare the statement of retained earnings before we prepare our balance sheet. I will show you how to prepare the statement of retained earnings later on. However, you need to get your figures right to have the balance sheet in a balanced state.

What exactly is owners' equity?

The owners' equity is the portion of the business that belongs to the owner. If you start a company with $3,000 from your personal savings, the entire business will be your property. At the end of the day, all the assets of the business will be equal to the owners' equity. However, if you get a loan of $1,000 to increase your assets, the net worth of your business will be $4,000, but your owners' equity will remain $3,000. In other words, the remaining part of the business is a liability, which cannot be termed as your property.

However, the owners' equity grows over time. For instance, in the example above, if you manage to repay your loan at the rate of $300 per year over 2 years, your owner's equity will increase. If the company assets are still worth $4,000 after those 2 years, your owners' equity will have increase from $3,000 to $3,600. The money used to pay the loan is assumed to be retained earnings from the business, which helps grow the value of your equity.

Items that represent owners' equity on your balance sheet include:

- Common stock
- Treasury stock
- Retained earnings

Step 4: Compare the sum of assets versus the sum of liabilities and owners' equity.

After compiling all the assets, sum them up on the left-hand side of the balance sheet. Sum up your liabilities and owners' equity on the right hand of the balance sheet. Compare the sum of the assets to that of the liabilities and owners' equity to see if they are equal. In case they have disparities, go back to your ledger book to see if you have made any errors with your entries. See the example balance sheet below.

Assets		Liabilities and Owners' Equity	
Cash	$6,600	Liabilities	
Accounts Receivable	$6,200	Notes Payable	$5,000
Tools and equipment	$25,000	Accounts Payable	$25,000
		Total liabilities	$30,000
		Owners' equity	
		Capital Stock	$7,000
		Retained Earnings	$800
		Total owners' equity	$7,800
Total	$37,800	Total	$37,800

Preparing the (P&L) Profit/Loss Statement

The profit/loss statement, also known as the income sheet, is a document that summarizes the revenue and expenses of a business over a given trading period. The income sheet is a very important document to the management of the business. It helps determine the current costs, their implications, and the possible ways of improving the profitability of a business.

Any accountant should be able to prepare a profit/loss statement whenever requested. Although the profit and loss statements are usually prepared alongside the balance sheet, you may want to prepare yours some months early. Here is a simple step by step guide on how to prepare a profit and loss statement.

Step 1: Determine the gross revenue.

From your ledger book, pull out every entry that represents revenue. This is the only way you will be able to determine the total income of your business.

Some of the entries that may represent revenue include:

- Cash sales
- Accounts receivable
- Cash at hand, etc.

However, you should be careful not to use the same value twice when determining your total revenue. For instance, if all your sales entries are deposited in the bank account, only use the "cash in bank" value to represent sales. You should not add the "cash sales" and "cash in the bank" amounts together.

Ensure that all the money that comes into the business through the selling of products and services is noted down. Further, you should remember that revenues that are not related to the daily operations of a business are not considered when preparing the profit and loss statement.

In other words, if you sell a company van that has been in use for years, you do not record it as revenue in the profit and loss statement. You only record revenue received from the sale of products and services.

Step 2: Determine the direct costs and gross profit.

The second step involves compiling all your direct costs. Direct costs represent the expenses that directly contribute to the value of a product.

In production, direct costs may include the cost of raw materials, direct labor, etc. In retail, direct costs primarily represent the cost of the product to be sold. For you to determine the gross profit your business makes, you should subtract direct costs from the total revenue.

Gross Profit = Total Revenue - Direct costs

When preparing an income sheet, the items on your summary document are made systematically. We start by registering the total revenue of the business and systematically break down the costs until we arrive at the net income of the business.

You can see from the income sheet templet below that, each section allows you to sum up the items.

After determining the gross profit, you should use the value obtained to calculate the gross margin. The gross margin is basically the gross profit depicted in percentage.

Converting this figure into percentage makes it easy for external users to interpret the profitability of the business.

Income Statement

For the Period Ended _____

Revenue	20__	20__
Sales Revenue		
(Less Sales Returns and Allowances)		
Service Revenue		
Interest Revenue		
Other Revenue		
Total Revenues	$ 000000	$ 0000000
Expenses		
Advertising		
Bad Debts		
Commissions		
Cost of Goods Sold		
Depreciation		
Employee Benefits		
Furniture and Equipment		
Insurance		
Interest Expense		
Maintenance and Repairs		
Office Supplies		
Payroll Taxes		
Rent		
Research and Development		
Salaries and Wages		
Software		
Travel		
Utilities		
Others		
Total Expenses	$ 000000	$ 0000000
Net Income Before Taxes	$ 000000	$ 00000
Income Tax Expense		
Income from Continuing Expenses		
Below-the-Lined Items		
Income from Discounted items		
Effect of Accounting Changes		
Extra Ordinary Items		
Net Income		

Gross Margin = (Gross Profit/ Gross Revenue) x 100

For example, if you sell cooking pans, you have to purchase them at a lower price and sell at a slightly higher price to make a profit. Let's say you purchased 100 pans at $50 each and sell all the pans at the price of $60 each. In this case, your direct cost would be the cost of buying the pans, your total revenue would be the amount sold for the pans, and your gross profit would be the difference between total revenue and direct costs.

Direct costs would be 50 x 100= $5,000

Total revenue would be 60 x 100= $6,000

Gross profit would be $6000 - $5000 = $1,000

Gross margin would be (1000/5000) x 100 = 20%

The gross margin of a business indicates its stability. If your accountant gives you the income statement without calculating the gross margin, you could simply do the calculations yourself. If your business is performing well, you will have a higher gross margin value.

Step 3: Calculate the Earnings Before Interest and Taxes (EBIT).

Earnings Before Interest and Taxes (EBIT) is a value that represents the gross profit, less operating expenses. Operating expenses (OPEX) represent all the costs incurred in the process of production, marketing, and selling a product that cannot be directly traced to the final product.

Operating expenses may include:

- Rent
- Labor
- Transportation
- Electricity
- Other utilities

EBIT = Gross profit - Operating expenses

Step 4: Calculate the Earnings Before Tax (EBT)

The earnings before tax is a figure that provides a clear picture of your business's performance. The EBT represents the actual gross profit of a business since it is the true income. If you do not deduct operating expenses from your gross profit, you may end up with a false net income at the end of the trading period.

EBT= EBIT- Depreciation

Step 5: Calculate your tax to get your net income.

After determining your earnings before tax, you need to calculate the taxes and deduct them to get your net income. The value of tax you pay depends on the type of business, the location of your business, and taxing policies in your locality.

There are some businesses that have to pay taxes to local authorities, while others only have to pay taxes to the federal government.

After deducting all the necessary taxes from your income, the remaining amount will represent your net income.

Net profit/loss = EBT - Taxes

Sales		$50,00,000
Cost of Goods Sold		
Materials	8,00,000	
Labor	11,00,000	
Overhead	6,00,000	25,00,000
Gross Margin		**$25,00,000**
Operating Expenses		
Selling Expenses	9,00,000	
Administrative Expenses	6,00,000	
Depreciation and Amortization	5,00,000	2000000
Operating Income		**$5,00,000**
Other Income & Expenses		
Interest Revenue	50000	
Interest Expense	-1,00,000	
Extraordinary items	2,00,000	1,50,000
Income Before Tax		**$6,50,000**
Income Tax (at 35%)		$2,27,500
Net Income		**$4,22,500**

As you can see from my profit and loss statement above, we have calculated the value of taxes and subtracted from the EBT value to determine the net profit. There are several approaches that you can take when preparing your profit and loss statement. You could choose to break your expenses down as we have done, or you could just sum up all your expenses and deduct them from your revenue to determine the net profit. However, breaking your figures down is necessary for those who may want to use your statements.

Preparing the Statement of Cash Flow

The statement of cash flow is another important financial statement that is used for internal monitoring. The statement can also be used by creditors and investors who may want to partner with your business. Preparing the statement of cash flow does not require much except for the general ledger and income sheet.

In the simplest terms possible, the statement of cash flow is a summary of the money that comes in and goes out. If you are running a business, you have to spend money, earn money, borrow money, and lend money. The statement of cash flow tries to account for the movement of money in these directions. Without the statement of cash flow, it is impossible to determine the performance of a business. It is through this statement that we can tell whether the business has enough funds to manage its activities.

The statement of cash flow takes care of 3 key aspects. It accounts for operating activities cash flow, which is the money that flows in and out of the business due to maintaining day to day operations. The operating activities cash flow accounts for direct expenses such as the cost of materials and direct revenue, such as cash sales. It is such items that determine the sustainability of the business in the short term.

Secondly, the statement of cash flow has to account for investing activities cash flow. These include long-term activities that generate money for the business. For example, if your business invests in market securities, long terms assets, and such activities, they are recorded under investing activities.

Lastly, a statement of cash flow has to account for financing activities. Financing activities cash flow refers to transactions between a company and its owners, creditors, and external investors. For example, if the owner invests more capital or takes dividends out of the business, it is considered financing activities cash flows. Understanding these three key areas of your cash flow statement is paramount. You should be able to group all your transactions as operating, financing, or investing activities. After categorizing all your transactions, you can prepare your statement of cash flow.

You should prepare your statement of cash flow at the end of the trading period. When you prepare your balance sheet, income sheet, and owner equity statements, it is advisable to also prepare a statement of cash flow.

There are two methods of preparing the statement of cash flow. We could use the direct or indirect methods of preparation. The method of preparation you choose will determine how detailed your statement should be. The direct method tends to focus more on the details than the indirect method. Since the indirect method is much easier for beginners, it is favorable for the readers of this book. Here is a step by step guide to preparing the statement of cash flow using the indirect method.

Step 1: Gather all transactions from the ledger book.

Since a statement of cash flows is only prepared within a given trading period, the first step should involve gathering all the necessary data from the general ledger. The general ledger records the summaries of all transactions that a company undertakes. If you want to prepare your statement of cash flow, the important document you will need is a general ledger that has been thoroughly audited. The other important document you will use in this process is the profit and loss statement. Gather all the transactions that represent revenue and expenses from your ledger book.

Step 2: Calculate cash flow from operating activities.

Once you have the above two documents on the table, use them to make calculations for the various cash flow activities. Positive cash flow, which is money entering the business, is recorded as plain figures while negative cash flow, which is money leaving the business, is recorded in brackets.

To calculate the cash flow from operating activities, you have to start by obtaining the value of Earnings Before Interest and Taxes (EBIT).

Cash flow from operating activities = EBIT + Depreciation

When calculating the value of depreciation, you consider the market value of an asset currently versus the value of the same product at the time it was purchased. If you bought a company van 5 years ago, the value of the van has probably reduced. When determining the cash flow for a certain trading period, we must add the total sum of depreciation within a given trading period.

Step 3: Determine investing activities and calculate investing activities cash flow.

The investments you make are meant to generate profits. However, in some cases, even long-term investments may lead to losses. Investing activities cash flow helps determine the profitability of your investments. For instance, if you buy a new asset, you give out cash. This transaction is registered as a negative cash flow. On the other hand, if you collect the money given out as a loan or if you sell an old asset, you gain cash. This transaction can be termed as positive cash flows.

To determine your investing cash flows, just subtract your outflow investments from your inflow investments. You will determine whether you are experiencing positive or negative investing cash flows. It is important to note that investing cash flows may be negative when your business is making a profit. Cash flows are mainly focused on the long-term benefits of the business.

Step 4: Determine financing activities cash flow.

After calculating operating and investing cash flows, determine the financing cash flows. Financing cash flows include long-term funding received from investors or your personal account. Negative financing cash flow can refer to activities such as collecting dividends, paying long-term loans, paying creditors, etc.

After calculating the three types of cash flow, sum them up to determine the overall cash flow of your business. Remember that some of the cash flow figures might be negative. If the figure is negative, you subtract instead of adding.

	$
CASH FLOW FROM OPERATING ACTIVITIES	
Cash receipts from customers (10,500 + 5,000)	15,500
Cash paid to suppliers and employees (4,000 + 200)	(4,200)
Cash generated from operations	11,300
Net cash flow from operating activities	11,300
CASH FLOW FROM INVESTING ACTIVITIES	
Additions to equipment	(12,000)
Net cash flow from investing activities	(12,000)
CASH FLOW FROM FINANCING ACTIVITIES	
Proceeds from capital contributed	15,000
Drawings	(500)
Proceeds from loan	5,000
Payment of loan	(4,000)
Net cash flow from financing activities	15,500
NET INCREASE/DECREASE IN CASH	14,800
Cash at the beginning of the period	-
Cash at the end of the period	14,800

Preparing the Statement of Retained Earnings

The statement of retained earnings is a document that is used by investors and the company owners. In most cases, retained earnings are reinvested in the business.

Retained earnings outline the changes in owners' equity. Most people confuse retained earnings for owners' equity. Although retained earnings can be part of the owner's equity, it is not the same as owners' equity. If you get a positive retained earnings figure, you can add it to your owners' equity, but if you get a negative retained earnings value, you subtract it from the owner's equity.

As we have already seen, owners' equity represents the portion of the business that can be claimed by the owner. If your small business was to be dissolved today, whatever you can rightfully claim as your own is the value of the owner's equity. However, retained earnings represent the growth in owners' equity over the lifespan of a business.

Example:

If you started your business 10 years ago with a capital of $4,000 and a loan of $6,000, your business's net worth was $10,000 at the time of start. At the same time, your owners' equity was just $4,000, because it was your stake in the business. However, if you have managed to clear your loans over the past ten years, and your business is still worth $10,000, your owners' equity has grown from $4,000 to $10,000. This growth can be attributed to retained earnings.

The assumption here is that the profit you were making over the years was used to clear the loan. Whether you collected some dividends or not, the rest of the profits was used to clear the debts, and now you have 100% ownership of the business. We can, therefore, say that your retained earnings over the past 10 years are $6,000.

Retained earnings are calculated cumulatively. Assuming that your retained earnings for the past 10 years are $6,000 as we have seen above, what will be your retained earnings at the end of this year? If you make a profit, you may record a positive retained earnings figure by adding your retained income for this year to your previous retained earnings.

What is the purpose of retained earnings?

When money is earned in your business, you could choose to use it all for personal purposes. This is what we refer to as collecting dividends. When a business makes a net profit, other expenses such as dividends are subtracted from the net profit; if there is a surplus amount left, it is categorized as retained earnings.

Retained earnings can be used for many purposes in a business. If you have earned substantial surplus income, you may use it to expand the business. You can choose to increase the branches', double production capacity, or launch a new product.

Further, you may use the value of retained earnings to bargain for possible mergers. If the company is operating as a publicly-traded entity, common stockholders can use retained earnings to buy back some shares of the business.

The statement of retained earnings is an important document because it helps us calculate owners' equity. As I have mentioned above, you cannot prepare your balance sheet unless you know the retained earnings value. You should first calculate your retained earnings before you start preparing your balance sheet.

Retained Earnings = Beginning Balance of RE + Net (Profit/loss) - Dividends

As you can see from the formula above, retained earnings are determined by adding the current retained earnings to the balance of retained earnings from the previous trading period.

For instance, if the value of retained earnings from the previous trading period is $4,000 and you make a net income of $1,000 and have to pay dividends worth $600, your retained earnings figure will be.

$4,000 + ($1,000-$600) = $4,400

The value of retained earning obtained should help you calculate owners' equity. As we have already discussed above, owners' equity represents the section of the business that belongs to the owner.

In other words, owners' equity represents all the assets of the business that you can claim for yourself in a sole proprietorship.

Owners' equity = Capital + Total Retained Earnings

This is the simplest way to calculate owners' equity in a sole proprietorship. If you have been running a small business, there are only two ways you can invest in your business: through direct capital injection or by reinvesting retained earnings. You can also calculate owners' equity by subtracting liabilities from assets.

Owners' equity = Assets - Liabilities

As we have already discussed above, every property of the business (assets) is acquired by money invested by the owners (capital + retained earnings) or money borrowed (liabilities).

Understanding this concept will make managing your business much easier. You can easily determine your stake in a business, prepare your balance sheet, and reduce your liabilities.

How to Interpret Financial

Statements

If you are an owner or manager of a business, your biggest worry is not preparing financial statements but rather interpreting them. You should be able to interpret all the major financial statements for various reasons. First, you have to interpret your financial statements for internal use. It is not possible for any business to benefit from the financial statements unless the data is utilized in making investment decisions.

Secondly, you should understand the financial statements of other businesses that you work with. If you are going to offer products on credit or get into investment agreements, you should make decisions based on financial data.

Besides your need for financial statements, many other individuals can benefit from the financial statements produced by your company. In some instances, you may be required to provide the data within your financial statements by compulsory. Here are some of the uses of financial statements.

How to Use the Balance Sheet

A balance sheet can be used by the company, investors, lenders, customers, and suppliers. Some of the key uses of the balance sheet include:

To determine if working capital is enough. The balance sheet is the only financial statement that allows you to see your financial position clearly. The most important aspect of a balance sheet is the fact that it shows your current working capital and the general growth of a business.

Working capital is the amount of cash held in liquid assets that can easily be used to run day-to-day operations.

Working Capital = Current assets - Current liabilities

Through the balance sheet, you can determine the sustainability of your business model and determine your capital needs. If your current liabilities override current assets, you need to find a way of injecting fresh capital into the business.

To know the business's net worth. The information about the net worth of a company can be beneficial to the owners, potential investors, lenders, and the government. Just by looking at a balance sheet, you can determine the net worth of the business.

Business Net worth = Total assets - Total liabilities

As you can see from the equation above, the net worth of the business can also be termed as owners' equity. In a case where the business is a publicly-traded company, many people may have a stake in the net worth of a company. Therefore, the shareholders also need to know the net worth of the company.

To see if the company can sustain future operations. The other important factor that you can learn from a balance sheet is the sustainability of a business. A business might be performing very well-currently, but the future is bleak. The best indicator of the future is the long-term assets. As the manager of the business, you need to start looking at a way of ensuring that your business is sustainable.

For example, if you are running a coffee processing plant, your long-term assets include your machinery and premises. If you are making good profits this year, but your machines have outlived their life span or the lease has expired, chances are that you will have problems in the near future.

To identify if there's a possible issuance of dividends. Most business owners can only benefit from the business if there are retained earnings. In other words, the business should be able to generate income that the owners can share as dividends. If the value of retained earnings on the balance sheet is high, the owners make a hefty profit.

How to Use the Income Statement

The income statement, also known as the profit and loss statement, is vital to a business. It has plenty of uses for the business owners, investors, tax agencies, suppliers, and the press. Some of the uses include:

To determine the sales figures. This is a very important need for all businesses. The business owners and marketers need to determine the sales that are made over a given trading period. The sales figure represents the revenue generated.

To determine the cost of goods sold and set prices. Determining the cost of goods is very vital for the business. For you to be able to set the right prices, you need to determine the overall cost of goods. Government agencies that set standards and prices may also need your cost of goods.

To determine profits. The information obtained from your income statement can benefit your company and external investors. The profits of your company determine the amount of tax payable and also determine the dividends received by shareholders. For this purpose, you are supposed to share your income statement. Publicly traded companies are required by law to share income statements with shareholders and the tax authorities.

To manage operating expenses. Operating expenses refer to the costs of running day to day business that cannot be directly traced to the final product.

Operating expenses can be adjusted to reduce business expenses. Most businesses use the income statement to determine expenses that can be adjusted to facilitate smooth operations.

How to Use the Cash Flow Statement

The cash flow statement is a document that shows money coming in and going out of business. There are many uses for the statement of cash flow. Some of the uses include.

For a comparison of cash flow. If you are running a business, you may want to know if it is growing or diminishing. The statement of cash flow is very important to the board of management since it helps in comparing the cash flows of previous trading periods. In this manner, you can determine whether the business is growing or not.

To determine a firm's liquidity. Determining the liquidity of a business is vital for investors, lenders, and owners. The liquidity of a business is determined by the value of current assets. The current assets of a business will determine its sustainability in the short run. If you have a positive cash flow, the business is in a position to continue running without problems.

For planning the payment of loans. The other importance of the statement of cash flow to the owners is planning loan repayment. Loans are repaid over a long time, and the interest rates are paid over a given period, and the time required to pay the loan determines the interest rates. The statement of cash flow may give you an idea of whether your business is capable of servicing current loans. If so, you can even go ahead and take more loans to improve the performance of the business.

To determine eligibility for loans. When lenders are giving out loans, they look at the flow of cash in your business. The total revenue of business shows you whether your business is capable of paying its loans. The statement of cash flow helps you determine your available loans and the possibility of paying all the loans. With such information, lenders will choose to provide loans or reject.

How to Use the Statement of Retained Earnings

The statement of retained earnings is very important to business owners, prospective investors, shareholders, tax authorities, and the press. The statement of retained earnings shows the income of a business that is retained after paying taxes and dividends. Some of the uses of retained earnings include:

To determine the dividends. The statement of retained earnings helps shareholders to calculate expected dividends. Since publicly traded companies offer dividends based on the available income, the statement of retained earnings should be released to shareholders in time.

To determine the sustainability of a company. Investors who chose to partner with your business will want to consider your business's sustainability. The key issues to look at when determining sustainability include retained earnings, fixed assets, liquid assets, etc.

Chapter 4: Accounting Principles

In my introduction, I mentioned that anyone can account for their money. The only difference between a certified accountant and any other person is the ability to adhere to the set accounting standards. Accounting rules, guidelines, and principles form the backbone of the entire practice.

If you run a small business, you may not necessarily be required to follow all the set accounting principles. However, limited companies and large corporations are required by law to follow certain accounting principles. With that said, whether you run a small business or a large corporation, it is in your best interest to follow the set accounting rules and guidelines.

Accounting principles determine how you record your transactions and how you store them. They also determine the types of financial statements you prepare and how to use such statements. Besides the preparation of statements, you need your books of accounts when sourcing for financing. Your chance of getting a loan for your business depends on presenting files that follow all the accounting principles.

In essence, accounting guidelines and principles bring universality to all books of accounts. If you follow the prescribed accounting rules, your books and financial statements can easily be interpreted by an accountant from across the word. This makes it easy for lenders and tax authorities to audit your records. Further, you may want an auditor to look at your books for internal purposes. The books can only be audited if you follow the prescribed accounting standards.

In this chapter, we are going to look at the laws, rules, guidelines, and policies that govern accounting. Since accounting is a practice that touches the core of society, it is an area that is monitored by many parties. The Generally Accepted Accounting Principles GAAPs are the commonly referenced rules when we talk about accounting. The GAAPs are set by the Financial Accounting Standards Board (FASB).

The other body involved in setting accounting guidelines is the Accounting Standards Board (IASB), which sets the International Finance Accounting Standards (IFRS). The IFRS are just principles that govern accounting on a global scale. Lastly, other rules and regulations are set at regional and local levels by government agencies involved in tax collection, business registration, and product standardization. When you get into business, you should not only look at the GAAPs and IFRS, but you should also try to determine the local rules and guidelines that control accounting in your locality.

The 4 Principles of Financial Accounting

Accounting as a practice is built on 4 broad principles. As long as your books follow the four major principles of accounting, you are less likely to have problems with any agency. The basic principles of accounting include:

Cost Principle

The cost principle of accounting requires that the cost of assets recorded during the preparation of financial statements should be the actual cost and not based on the market value. This principle tries to discourage cases where businesses may inflate the prices of assets to increase expenditure. In case you are buying a used van for your business, you should record the cost of the van as it is instead of recording the market value of a new van.

This principle is sometimes referred to as the historical principle since the costs of assets are recorded at the time of purchase and not at the time of reporting. Even if you purchased an asset at the start of the fiscal year, you cannot record its cost as its market value at the end of the same year. You must infer to the buying cost and use the actual figure in your financial reports.

Revenue Principle

The revenue principle states that revenues should be recorded at the time they are earned, and not when payment is received. This principle of accounting gave birth to accounts receivables and accounts payables. It prevents errors occurring in accounting due to delayed payments. All the money owed to your business is deemed as money belonging to the business.

With that said, this principle does not affect the cash method of accounting as long as all revenues are recognized once they are received. For the cash method of accounting, revenues are only recognized once money changes hands. This is acceptable as long as the revenue is recognized as soon as the transaction is deemed complete. The cash method of accounting can only be used by small businesses with less than $1 million in annual revenue.

Matching Principle

The matching principle requires that expenses are matched with the revenue they are related to. This principle of accounting eliminates the instances where a company spends money on items that do not associate with its production. Expenses should not just be recorded because they happened but because they contribute to the revenue of the business.

With the matching principle, it is easy to evaluate the profitability of goods and services. We can easily track the cost of goods, direct expenses, and distinguish them from indirect expenses. It is important to note that some expenses, such as labor costs, electricity costs, etc., cannot be directly linked with the revenue of the business. Therefore, they are just recorded as expenses for the current period.

Disclosure Principle

Lastly, the principle of disclosure requires that all the financial information disclosed by a business should be released in a form that is easy to understand. This explains the reason why companies have to prepare financial statements at the end of each trading period. It is through such summarized documents that the outside world gets to see what happens inside a business.

If any information is needed to explain certain figures on the summary documents, it must be provided in the body of the statement. Further, the amount of information provided should be sufficient for cooperative executives to make a decision.

12 Concepts of GAAP

The Generally Accepted Accounting Principles (GAAP) are the commonly referenced standards when making entries in journals, ledgers, and preparing financial statements. The GAAPs are used in the US mostly, with little reference to IFRS principles. The generally accepted principles are built upon 12 key concepts of accounting.

Any accountant with an understanding of these 12 concepts should be able to prepare financial reports that are universal. All bookkeepers should also follow these principles to avoid inconsistencies within the books. Here are the 12 concepts of accounting.

Accounting Entity

An accounting entity refers to the business unit for which accounting is done. This concept recognizes that a business is a separate entity from its owners. This principle of accounting makes it easy to separate the money belonging to a business from the cash that belongs to the owners. This is a concept that most small business owners fail to recognize and end up making accounting errors.

Going Concern

This concept recognizes that the life of a business is infinitely long and that the business is less likely to be closed. Even if the business may go bankrupt, the accountant must give a qualified opinion stating that the business might not survive. This concept makes it possible for a business to operate, even if it has more liabilities than assets.

Measurement

This concept of accounting only recognizes things that are quantifiable. Therefore, aspects that are not measured or quantifiable, such as customer loyalty, may not be accounted for. Although goodwill is recognized as an asset, it might not capture all the things that are not quantifiable in a business.

Units of Measure

This concept recognizes one unit of measurement over the lifespan of a business. If you are operating your business in the US, the USD is the standard unit of measurement. If you are operating in any other country, you may use your local currency or other international currencies.

The only problem would be if you choose to use more than one unit of measurement in your books. This means that even if you run an international business, you cannot use both the USD and Euro in your books. You have to choose one unit of measurement and work with it throughout.

Historical Cost

This infers to the cost principle, which states that the value of an asset recorded should be the actual value at the time of purchase and not according to current market value. If you purchased a piece of land at $5,000 in January and the land losses value due to inflation in December to $4,000, you must record the value of the land as $5,000.

Materiality

The concept of materiality allows the accountant to violate other accounting principles. For instance, if the value of an entry is so small that the financial reports would not have an impact, the accountant may leave it out. This concept allows the accountant to make the judgment call. Although this concept is a loophole for accounting malpractices, it is also vital in ensuring that all accounting reports are relevant and informational.

Estimates and Judgments

The concept of estimates and judgments allows the accountant to guess figures that will not significantly affect the financial reports. For instance, if you purchased a car but the transaction cannot be traced in your financial documents, the accountant may choose to guess the price of the car according to the estimated market value and include it. This concept is only allowed due to the complex nature of the business and should not be taken for granted.

Consistency

The concept of consistency requires that each business entity maintains consistency in the system of accounting. If you are using the double-entry method of bookkeeping, you are required to stick to it throughout. If you are using the accrual method of bookkeeping, you are also required to stick to it. This helps ensure that there is consistency throughout your records. If you have to change some of your reporting patterns, you are required to notify your local tax agencies.

Conservatism

This principle states that if doubt exists between two alternatives, an accountant must choose the result with lesser profit. For instance, if you are doubting the credibility of two figures recorded in your books of account. You are required to pick a figure that reduces the income of the company or one that leads to less profit.

Periodicity

This concept requires that accounting is done within a given period. For instance, the financial statements are prepared annually, semi-annually, or quarterly.

The lifespan of a business is divided into such periods for easy accounting. If we were to account for the lifespan of a business after a very long time, we would miss very many figures, and errors can easily compile.

Substance Over Form

This concept of accounting requires that each item is accounted for according to its economic substance and not form. In other words, we account for an asset according to the value it adds to the business and not just based on its market value.

Accrual Basis of Presentation

The concept of accrual accounting requires that if a business makes a transaction within a given trading period, then it must be recorded within the same period. This concept mainly applies to businesses that keep inventory. For instance, if you supply goods on credit on December 31st this year, you must record the goods within the transactions of the current year, even if they will be paid for in January.

The revenue recorded in accrual accounting may not be received, and the expenses recorded may not be paid.

The opposite of accrual accounting is cash basis accounting. Businesses that do not have inventory are allowed to use the cash basis bookkeeping. In this method, transactions are only recorded once they are completed. In other words, once cash changes hands.

What is the accounting equation?

The accounting equation is the basis upon which the double-entry system is founded. The accounting equation balances the entire company's assets and liabilities. The equation states that the company assets must equal the sum of liabilities and shareholders' equity.

In the previous chapter, we have explained the relationship between shareholders' equity, liabilities, and assets. As we have seen, all the assets of a company are acquired by the capital invested by the owners, money borrowed, or profits that are plowed back into the business. This concept gives us the accounting equation.

Based on the double-entry system of accounting, the balance sheet must always be balanced. The items on the left-hand side (assets) and the items on the right-hand side (liabilities + owner's equity) must always balance.

The double entry system requires that every entry that is made on the debit side of the ledger is replicated with an equal and opposite entry on the credit side. This way, the entries on the debit and credit side must balance (trial balance). The trial balance shows the cumulative credit and debit transactions of the business over the trading period in question. This way, we can establish the authenticity of all the transactions within the given trading period.

The accounting equation formula:

Assets = Liabilities + Owner's Equity

Since the accounting equation is based on the balance sheet, you need to bring all the items needed for a balance sheet on the table. To calculate the accounting equation, determine all the assets on the balance sheet, and get the total. After determining your total assets, add up the liabilities too, and get the total liabilities.

While assets and liabilities can easily be traced even from your ledger book, you need to calculate shareholder's equity independently. To determine the owners' equity, add your retained earnings for the current trading period to your shareholders' equity at the start of the trading period.

Owners' Equity = Owners Equity Carried Forward + Retained Earnings

To determine whether the accounting equation is accurate, sum up the liabilities and owners' equity. If the sum of your liabilities and owners' equity is equal to the sum of assets, your balance sheet is accurate.

Let's say for the fiscal year ending 2019, Melisa Holdings reported the following figures:

- Total assets $170 million
- Total liabilities $120 million
- Owners' equity $50 million

If we use the equation *Assets = liabilities + owners' equity*, we should say that $170 = ($50 + $120). As you can see from the example above, all assets add up to $170, and the liabilities summed up with owners' equity also add up to $170.

What do the items in the equation mean?

Most people are unable to interpret what these items truly represent in a real business environment. If you cannot distinguish assets, liabilities, and owners' equity, this equation may be of little help.

Assets

Assets are all the properties owned by the business, including cash and cash equivalents. The term asset simply refers to something of value that a person or a business owns. If you own a house, it is your asset because it is an item of value. Assets increase the value of the company and may not be something tangible.

Although most people think that an asset must be something tangible, assets can be in the form of cash or goodwill. For instance, accounts receivable are listed as assets in accounting. Although the money listed under accounts receivable is yet to be received, it is perceived as an asset of the business.

Liabilities

In accounting, liabilities refer to all entries that reduce the value of a business or a company. In simple terms, liabilities refer to what a business owes other businesses of individuals. For example, if you borrow a long-term loan, the loan becomes a liability. The loan is not an asset to the company but a liability. Since assets improve the value of the business, while liabilities reduce the value of a business, the true value of any business is deemed as the difference between assets and liabilities.

Shareholders' Equity

Owners' equity represents the portion of a company that is owned by the shareholders. Owners' equity can be calculated by subtracting liabilities from total assets. However, this is only applicable in a case where the balance sheet has already been prepared. If the balance sheet is yet to be prepared, you can determine shareholders' equity by adding retained earnings to the value of shareholders' equity brought forward from the previous trading period.

Retained earnings refer to the portion of net income that is not paid out to shareholders as dividends. After deducting taxes from the gross income, the remaining income is known as net Income. The shareholders receive dividends according to the agreed method of distribution, but a portion of the income is retained in the business. The retained portion is what we call retained earnings and is always added to the owners' equity.

How do you apply the accounting equation?

The accounting equation can be applied to any business. It serves the same purpose across the board for both small and large businesses. However, the way the equation is implemented depends on the ownership structure of a business. Here is the way you need to apply the equation, depending on your business structure.

Applying the Accounting Equation to Corporations

A corporation is a large and complex business entity that has complex transactions. In theory, a corporation does not have an owner but shareholders. There are two types of shareholders (common stockholders and preferred stockholders). The common stockholders often represent the largest shareholders in the business and sometimes the founders of the business. Common stockholders have a say in the decisions of the business and can make key changes to the way the business is run.

When applying the accounting equation to a corporation, you should keep in mind the fact that the business assets are not owned by anyone. The corporation is seen as an entity that can sue and be sued. In other words, the shareholders only claim the owners' equity section of the business and not the assets. Secondly, the earnings of a corporation are first distributed to preferred shareholders before the common shareholders get a claim. After preferred and common shareholders get their portion, the remaining amount is reinvested into the business as retained earnings.

Applying the Accounting Equation to an LLC

A limited liability company LLC is a business where the company is owned by the members. The ownership of an LLC can be expressed in 2 ways; by percentage or by owners units. If you start a limited company with 9 other individuals, you may choose to contribute 10% of the assets each and hold a 10% stake each. Unlike it is the case with corporations, an LLC can distribute its interests as it pleases.

When applying the accounting equation to an LLC, there should be an agreement between the members. The members should decide who gets the largest portion of the earnings and what happens to retained earnings. Besides the distribution of retained earnings, the assets of the business should equal the sum of liabilities and owner's equity as it is the case with corporations.

Applying the Accounting Equation in a Partnership

A partnership is a business that is owned by two or more members. There are different types of partnerships, and the type of partnership determines how to apply the accounting equation. For instance, a general partnership involves a case where two people come together to start a business.

The other type of partnership is a limited liability partnership, where the owners of the business operate it as an LLC. In an LLC partnership, the owners are called members and are not liable for the financial obligations of the business.

The accounting equation gets complicated when we come to a general partnership. The partners of the business should set the terms of their operations, asset ownership, and revenue distribution.

If the partnership is operated as an LLC, the assets are owned by the business, and the members-only get to claim the shares of owners' equity. However, if it is a general partnership, the members can lay claim to certain assets and may dissolve the business if one partner chooses to step out. Most importantly, members of a general partnership can be held liable for the debts of the business.

Applying the Accounting Equation to a Sole Proprietorship

Lastly, the accounting equation can be applied to a sole proprietorship. A sole proprietorship is simply a business that is owned and managed by a single person. To apply the accounting equation to a sole proprietorship, you should first recognize your business as an independent entity. If you mix your personal finances and business finances, it will be impossible to apply the accounting equation. In the application of the accounting equation, the assumption is that the assets of a sole proprietorship are owned by the business owner. In the same way, the liabilities of the business also fall on the owner of the business. If your business is unable to fulfill its obligations, your personal properties can be used to pay off the debts of the business.

Chapter 5: Financial Statements Analysis and Analysis Tools

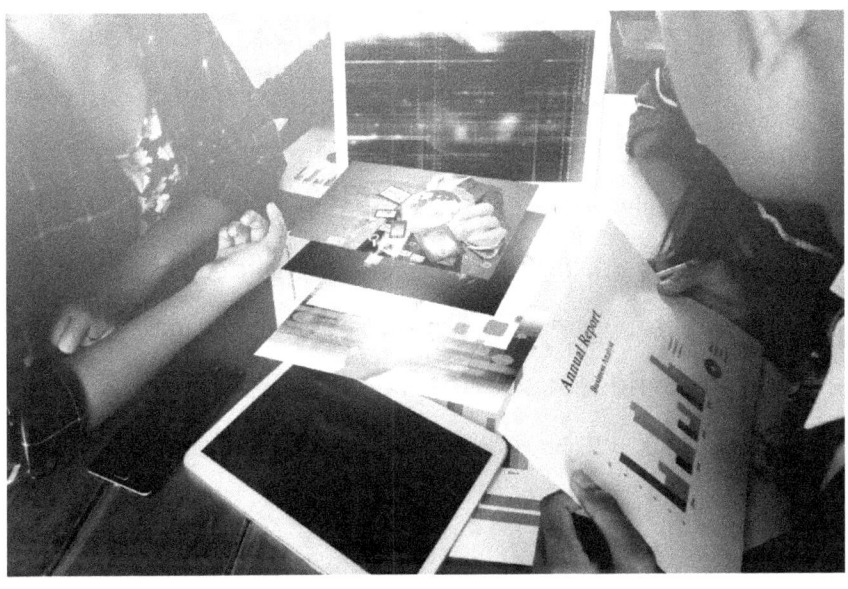

Besides bookkeeping and preparing financial statements, accounting also involves the preparation and interpretation of analysis tools. The financial statements prepared in the previous chapters do not show the position of a business comprehensively. Statements such as the balance sheet, profit and loss, and cash flow statements are of more help to the outside world than they are of help to the internal users without analytical tools.

The board of management, marketing departments, and branding departments of the company need more information. They need to find more detailed information that outlines the growth of the business and shows the differences in production, sales, and assets over time. Such analytical information is more vital in making key production, branding, and marketing decisions. Before any business chooses to expand, the necessary analytical tools must be reviewed. So, what exactly are financial analysis tools, and why do we need them?

Analysis Tools Used in Accounting

As we have seen from the chapters above, financial statements contain all the needed information about the assets, liabilities, revenues, expenses, and equity of a business. By looking at your balance sheet alone, you can determine the assets, liabilities, and owners' equity of a business.

If you look at the profit and loss statement, you can determine the net profit taxes, operational costs, direct costs, total revenue, etc. Although all these figures can easily be pulled out of the key financial statements, analyzing these statements is never easy. To simplify the analysis of financial statements, we use analysis tools. Analysis tools further break down the data into simple chunks that we can easily interpret.

For example, if I were to tell you that the owner's equity of a business is $5,000, you would not understand whether this is a big company or small company in terms of assets. However, if I told you that the owners' equity is $5,000, which is equal to 1/5 of the total assets, you can easily conceptualize how big the business is. This statement alone gives you an idea that the company has more liabilities than assets.

There are 4 broad categories of analysis tools that are used in interpreting financial statements. They include:

Comparative Statements

Comparative statements help in analyzing financial statements in a horizontal manner. In other words, they help you determine the financial position of business over two or more trading periods. The comparative tools help in comparing your cash flow from one period to another. If you can compare the assets of your company in two or three consecutive periods, you may be able to spot increases or decline in assets, liabilities, or owners' equity. Such analysis will help determine whether the business is growing, declining, or stagnant.

Common Size Statements

This refers to a vertical analysis of financial statements. In common size analysis, the assumption is that reading the actual figures can be misleading. If you make a profit of $1 million within a given trading period, you may think that the company is doing well. However, vertical analysis tries to compare the profit versus the investment in the income sheet. Further, you can compare your assets in terms of percentage to determine the true financial position of the business. In common size analysis, all the entries are regarded as being 100%, despite their magnitude.

In common size analysis, the entire balance sheet is converted into a percentage. The converted balance sheet is referred to as a common size balance sheet because all the items on the balance sheet can be interpreted as being of common size.

Trend Analysis

Besides common size tools, we can also analyze the trend in financial statements. Trend analysis, or what's commonly known as the pyramid analysis, helps study operational and financial results over a series of years. In trend analysis, the various items in financial statements are represented in the form of ratios.

Whether the enterprise is trending upwards or backward, trend analysis will help you see the real picture and make informed decisions. Trend analysis tools are very crucial to the management of the business as well as the outsiders.

Ratio Analysis

Ratio analysis refers to analytical tools that compare items on financial statements quantitatively. Ratio analysis simply describes the relationship which exists between several items on the financial statement. For example, we can say that the ratio of revenue to direct costs is 3:1. This way, we can see that the company is already making thrice the amount it spends on production. Even if you are not an expert at reading numbers, you can easily establish that the company is making a profit.

To help you understand the various analytical tools used in interpreting financial statements, let us look at the key tools used in accounting.

Liquidity Ratios

Liquidity ratios refer to a company's ability to clear its debt obligations when they are due. In other words, the liquidity ratio shows how quickly a company can convert its current assets into cash to payout current liabilities. As we have already mentioned, any company that has more current liabilities than current assets is likely to have problems in the near future.

The liquidity ratio tries to establish that a company is prepared enough to take care of current liabilities.

Why liquidity ratios?

The liquidity ration of a company affects its debt credibility. If your liquidity ratio is poor, it means that you are not in a position to clear your current debts in time. If this is the case, you may never be able to secure goods on credit or even obtain financing. Poor liquidity ratio simply shows that your business has cash flow problems.

Continuous failure to meet your short term obligations might lead the company to be declared bankrupt. The liquidity ratio is, therefore, vital in determining the financial stability of a business.

Types of Liquidity Ratios

Under the liquidity ratios financial analysis tools, there are several ratios that help determine the financial stability of the company.

The current ratio measures the overall financial strength of a company. The current ratio simply compares current assets to current liabilities. For you to say that a company is stable financially, the current assets should be more than the current liabilities.

Current ratio = Current assets / Current liabilities

The recommended current ratio is 2:1. Current assets represent all the items owned by a business that can be converted into cash in the near future. The items that make up current assets include cash, stock, loan advances, cash receivables, etc. The current liabilities, on the other hand, represent debts that should be paid in less than one year. The current liabilities of a company may include items such as creditors, short term loans, bank overdrafts, expenses, etc.

The acid test ratio or quick ratio is the second type of liquidity ratio. The acid test ratio compares current assets to current liabilities, except that the current assets are adjusted to eliminate those which are not in cash. For example, if you were to pay your debts within the next month, your current stock might not be very helpful. Instead of including stock in your current assets, the acid test ratio only accounts for the amount that is already available at hand and in the bank, cash receivable, and loans.

Acid Test Ratio = Quick Assets / Current Liabilities

To determine your quick assets, use the formula:

Quick assets = Current assets - Inventory - Prepaid Expenses

The absolute ratio is the third type of liquidity ratio. It only considers market securities and available cash at hand in determining the liquidity of the company.

Absolute Ratio = (Cash + Marketable Securities) / Current Liabilities

Lastly, the basic defense ratio defines the liquidity of a company. The basic defense ratio tries to show the exact number of days a company can cover its current obligations without needing external help. To determine your basic defense ratio, use the formula.

Basic Defense Ratio = (Cash + Receivables + Marketable Securities) ÷ (Operating expenses +Interest + Taxes) ÷ 365

Solvency Ratios

The solvency ratio, also known as the leverage ratio, determines a company's ability to meet its long term debt obligations. Unlike the liquidity ratio, the solvency ratio further focuses on the ability of a company to fully deal with its debt obligations. The solvency ratio of a company is very important to external investors.

If your company wants to get financial aid, you should prove that the business is in a position to repay the loan in the long run. The best way to determine whether a business is in a position to meet debt obligations is by looking at the solvency ratios. There are 4 solvency ratios that help us determine the viability of a business in terms of its financial strength.

Debt to Equity Ratio

The debt to equity ratio determines the relationship between long-term debts and the total equity of the firm.

Debt to equity = Long-term debt / Shareholders funds

Long-term debt = debentures + Long-term loans

Shareholders' Funds = Equity Share Capital + Preference Share Capital + Reserves – Fictitious Assets

The debt to equity ratio of a firm plays an important role in attracting investors. A low ratio means that the company has a stable financial base and can attract more investors. However, it also means that its equity is more diluted.

On the other hand, a high debt to equity ratio means that the company is riskier. The number of creditors may be more than investors, and such a business may turn away potential investors.

There are no industry measures that deter a company from obtaining more loans. As such, any business may easily find itself having more debts than equity.

However, it is recommended that every business should maintain a low debt to equity ratio as much as possible.

Debt Ratio

The debt ratio of a company compares its long-term debts to its capital. In other words, the debt ratio compares long term liabilities as a percentage of its net fixed assets.

Debt ratio = Long-term debt / Net assets

In this equation, net assets can also be referred to as capital employed. In other words, the net assets of a company represent the available working capital and are responsible for servicing long-term loans. The same equation can be represented as:

Debt ratio = Long-term debt / Capital employed

Capital Employed = Long Term Debt + Shareholders Funds

Net Assets = Non-Fictitious Assets – Current Liabilities

In the debt ratio, a low debt ratio indicates financial stability. If a firm has a low debt ratio, it attracts more creditors and investors. On the contrary, a high debt ratio may push away potential investors.

Proprietary Ratio

The proprietary ratio is the third solvency ratio. It represents the relationship between owners' equity and the capital employed.

Proprietary ratio = Owners equity / Net assets

If you get a high proprietary ratio, your business is running smoothly, and the finances are healthy. This means that a large portion of your company's assets is generated from owners' equity. As we have seen from the accounting equation, assets can only be acquired by money borrowed (liabilities), capital invested, or funds plowed back. If your business does not borrow money to purchases assets, the proprietary ratio will be high and will indicate a healthy business.

It is important to note that the sum of debt ratio and proprietary ratio should be 1. This is because the sum of debts (liabilities) and owners' equity should equal the sum of assets.

Interest Coverage Ratio

The interest coverage ratio is the fourth type of solvency ratio. It represents the comparison between the profits of a company and the interests payable on debts. If the profits generated by a company are low than the interest payable on loans, there are possible financial problems for the business.

Interest coverage ratio = Net Profit before Interest and Tax/ Interest on long-term debts

Profitability Ratios

Profitability ratios are used to analyze the profit and loss statements. They measure a company's ability to earn profits in relation to operating costs, sales revenue, and balance sheet assets. The profitability ratios show how well a company utilizes available assets and whether the assets will be profitable in the long run.

Just like it is the case with liquidity and solvency ratios, profitability ratios are also divided into categories. The various types of profitability ratios help us measure a company's financial performance with more accuracy and in diverse ways.

Margin Ratios

The first profitability ratio we look at is the margin ratio. Margin ratios examine the effectiveness of a company in transforming sales revenue into profit. There is a big difference between huge revenue and huge profits. A company may be making sufficient sales, but the resulting profit may not be sustainable. The margin ratio helps us determine the sustainability of the profit a company makes. Margin ratios are broken down into 3:

The gross profit ratio is the first profitability ratio that is calculated by any business. The gross profit ratio measures how much sales revenue remains after a company has covered its cost of goods (COGS).

The Gross Profit Margin = Gross profit / Sales revenue

The gross profit margin is represented in percentage. The higher the percentage, the better for your business. A higher percentage indicates that you have more money left for your business after deducting COGS from your total revenue.

The operating profit margin is the second type of margin ratios under profitability ratios. The operating profit margin represents the earnings before interest EBIT. To determine your operating profit margin, you have to deduct operating expenses from your gross profits. After deducting operation coasts, represent your EBIT value as a percentage of the total revenue. This helps to determine the percentage of revenue that remains after the COGS and OPEX have been deducted.

Operating profit margin = EBIT / Net sales

The operating margin can show us several things. If your operating margin is high, it shows that your business is healthy and that you are making profits. However, if your operating profit margin is low, there are two likely situations; either your gross profit margin is also low, or your operating costs are too high.

If you have a high gross profit margin, you should also have a high operating profit margin. However, if you spent too much on operational costs, your operating profit margin will be low. This kind of information should help you make informed decisions on the expenses to keep and the ones to cut down.

The last margin ratio is the net profit margin. This ratio represents the profitability of a business as a percentage of the total revenue. It reveals the amount of money your company makes and the amount that is retained as profits. The net profit margin shows the percentage of profit that is left after all expenses have been deducted. This includes depreciation and indirect expenses.

Net profit ratio = Net Income / Revenue

If you receive a high net profit ratio, your business is running well. However, a low net profit ratio may indicate that your business is straining. To improve your net profit ratio, you need to do proper bookkeeping so that you can reduce taxes, operational costs, and find a way of increasing the value of your products.

Return Ratios

The second type of ratio under profitability ratios is known as return ratio. The return ratio shows the profitability of a business to its owners and shareholders. There are two types of return ratios.

The first type of return ratio is the return on asset ratio. This type of return ratio shows how resilient your company is at turning its assets into profit. In other words, the return ratio shows how efficiently the company uses the available assets. If you use your assets accordingly, they will add value to your business and contribute to your profits. There are different ways of calculating return on investment ratios. The simplest formula for the return on investment ration is:

Return on assets = Net income / Total assets

The second return ratio is the return on equity ratio. This ratio shows how well a company uses shareholder's equity to generate income. It measures the shareholder's return on his/her investment.

Return on equity is always presented in percentage, and the higher the figure, the better. If you have a higher return on investment, your company gives confidence to external investors.

Return on equity = Net income/ Average shareholders' equity

Activity Ratios

The activity ratios are used to determine how efficient a business is running based on the available assets. They examine how actively assets of a company are used to generate revenue for the business. Activity ratios show how much sales have taken place in comparison to the assets available.

The activity ratio helps determine the efficiency in the management of assets. There are some assets of the company that may have little value to the business.

To determine the efficiency of your assets, you have to review the performance against the sales generated. There are seven types of activity ratios.

Total Assets Turnover Ratio

The total assets turnover ratio measures the overall efficiency in utilizing assets. A high ratio shows that a company is managing its assets efficiently in generating sales.

Total Asset Turnover Ratio = Sales / Total assets

Fixed Assets Turnover Ratio

This ratio shows the efficiency of a company in utilizing its fixed assets. Since fixed assets generate income slowly, it is important to ensure that they are truly profitable.

Fixed Asset Turnover Ratio = Total Sales / Fixed Assets

Current Assets Turnover Ratio

The current turnover ratio is a very important indicator that measures how well current assets are utilized in generating sales.

A high current assets turnover ratio shows that current assets such as cash are well managed and that they generate significant income.

Current Asset Turnover Ratio = Total Sales / Current Assets

Working Capital Turnover Ratio

This activity ratio shows how efficient the firm utilizes its working capital. As we have already seen, working capital refers to the assets that are available for productivity.

Working Capital Turn Over = Total Sales / Working capital

A higher ratio shows that the working capital is being utilized efficiently.

Stock Turnover Ratio

The stock turnover ratio describes the relationship between the cost of goods and the inventory.

This activity ratio aims at showing how fast the stock is being consumed. The stock turnover ratio is very vital in setting prices for the products.

A high stock turnover ratio indicates that the stock is being sold at a faster rate and is good for your business.

On the contrary, a low stock turnover ratio indicates that the goods being sold stay in the warehouse for a long time.

Stock Turnover Ratio = Cost of Goods Sold / Average Inventory

Average Inventory = (Opening Stock + Closing Stock) / 2

Debtor Turnover Ratio

The debtor turnover ratio helps the company determine debt collection efficiency. Debt collection can help a company meet its financial obligations if it is done in the right manner.

Through the debtor turnover ratio, a company can determine whether accounts receivable are being serviced or not.

Debt Turnover Ratio = Credit Sales / Average Debtors

Average Debtors = (Opening Debtor + Closing Debtor) / 2

Creditors' Turnover Ratio

The last activity ratio is the creditor turnover. This ratio helps determine the efficiency of paying company creditors. It shows the efficiency in managing accounts payable.

A high ratio shows the inability of a business to finance its credit purchases. This figure is very significant and may determine whether your creditors continue working with you.

If your business is not servicing the current credits, you may not be able to receive supplies from your creditors.

Creditors Turnover Ratio = Credit Purchases / Average Creditor

Average Creditors = (Opening Creditor + Closing Creditor)

Cash Flow Ratios

Cash flow ratios are vital analysis tools that help in interpreting the cash flow statement. The cash flow ratios compare the company's cash flow to revenue, assets, liabilities, and profits. Here are the main types of cash flow ratios.

Current Liability Coverage Ratio

The current liability coverage ratio is a cash flow ratio that measures the cash from operating activities. In other words, this ration compares cash from operating activities to current liabilities.

This ratio shows the ability of a company to generate enough cash to cover its current liabilities. Current liabilities are a company's obligations that should be resolved in the shortest time possible.

Current Liability Coverage Ratio = Net Cash from Operating Activities / Average Current Liabilities

Price to Cash Flow Ratio

The price to cash flow ratio is an estimate of the company's share prices to its cash flow. This method of determining the price of company shares is more acccpted than the price per earning approach. With the price to cash flow approach, it is harder for a company to make false internal adjustments.

Price to Cash Flow Ratio = Share Price / Operating Cash Flow per Share

The share price used in this formula is the closing price of the stock on a particular day or a certain trading period.

Cash Flow Margin Ratio

The cash flow margin is an important analysis tool for every business. It is an expression of the relationship between cash generated from operations and sales. It shows the amount of money generated per dollar of net sales.

Cash Flow Margin Ratio = Cash Flow from Operating Cash Flows / Net Sales

The figures for cash flow from operating cash flows can be found in your statement of cash flows, while the net sales can be found on your income sheet. The higher the percentage for this ratio, the better it is for your business.

Cash Flow Coverage Ratio

Lastly, the cash flow coverage ratio helps measure the solvency of the company. Just like the solvency ratio, the cash flow coverage ratio also determines the ability of a company to meet its long-term debts.

Cash Flow Converge Ratio = Cash Flow from Operations / Total Debt

The cash flow from operations figure can be acquired from your statement of cash flow while the total debt can be acquired from your balance sheet. The total debt represents total liabilities in your balance sheet.

A high cash flow coverage ratio shows that a company is able to pay its debts both short term and long-term. For a business to be deemed stable, a ratio of more than 1 is desired.

For example, if a company has an operating cash flow ratio of 1.5, it means that the company can pay its debts 1.5 times with the operating cash flows. In other words, if the company was required to clear all its debts instantly, it would clear them and remain with 0.5 of the amount used to clear the debt.

Coverage Ratios

Coverage ratios are used to determine whether a company can pay off its debt obligations. If the coverage ratio is high, it means that the company is healthy in terms of finances. If the ratio is low, it shows that the business is not in a position to fulfill debt obligations in due time. The coverage ratio compares a company's ability to cover its debts to other companies' ability to do the same. There are four types of coverage ratios.

Interest Coverage Ratio

The interest coverage ratio proves that a company can pay off its interests in debt using the earnings.

Interest Coverage Ratio = EBIT / Internet Expenses

Debt Service Coverage

The debt coverage ratio is used to examine the ability of a company to pay off its debt from its earnings. The interest coverage ratio determines the ability of a company to pay off its interests on debt while the debt service coverage determines the ability of a company to pay off the principal amount plus interest from its earnings.

If the debt service coverage ratio is more than 1, the company is in a good position to repay its loans.

Debt Service Coverage Ratio = Operating Income / Total Debt

Asset Coverage Ratio

The asset coverage ratio determines the capacity of a company to pay off its debt obligations from its assets. Unlike the debt service coverage ratio, the asset coverage ratio focuses on assets as the source of funds required to pay off its debts. The asset coverage ratio of a company can be used when determining the credit within your business. It is common for assets of a business to be sold off to pay debts in case a company is unable to fulfill its debt obligations.

Asset Coverage Ratio = (Tangible Asset – Short Term Liabilities) / Total Debt Operating Income / Total Debt

Cash Coverage Ratio

The cash coverage ratio is used to determine the ability of a company to pay off its interest obligations from the available cash. It is similar to the interest coverage ratio above, but instead of earnings, the interest is compared to the cash available. This means that the cash coverage ratio only considers the amount of money available on a specific date.

Accounting Software

The duties of an accountant are many, and they need the highest standards of accuracy. Traditionally, accountants had to maintain several books physically and make copies of their reports for security purposes. To ensure that all the data stored does not get lost, they had to photocopy documents and save similar softcopy files on more than one hard disk. However, bookkeeping and accounting are rapidly changing. Today, accountants and bookkeepers do not have to store paper files. Due to evolution in technology, there is little need for a bookkeeper to manually note down transactions.

Bookkeeping software makes it possible for transaction recording to be automated. For businesses that have gone paperless, the work of a bookkeeper can be handled with an automated system. In this manner, all sales figures are automatically recorded as soon as the transaction happens. The figures are then computed to produce financial reports.

Accounting software refers to programs that are used in bookkeeping, preparing financial reports, and analyzing these reports. Accountants across the world are required to be familiar with the latest accounting software. According to a study done by the Board of Certified Accountants, the most important skill for an accountant today is the ability to use accounting software. Most employers are looking for accountants who are tech-savvy to help push the agenda of the business using technology.

Accounting software makes the work of an accountant much easier. With accounting software, most of the data entry tasks are automated. Further, most programs come with ready templates to help in preparing financial reports. After preparing financial reports, a simple command can help you generate all the analytical tools we have looked at. With accounting software, you can easily process payroll, file your taxes, and monitor the growth of your business.

There are many accounting software options to choose from. From the basic Microsoft Excel to more complex programs such as QuickBooks, you have plenty of options to choose from. The choice of accounting software you make depends on your technological know-how, the amount you are willing to invest, and your accounting skills. Some programs can handle almost everything there is pertaining to accounting. Your only duty is to provide the necessary data. Here are some of the best accounting programs and their benefits.

Microsoft Excel

Microsoft Excel is probably the oldest accounting software. It is the one software that made accounting much simple by providing options to save accounting data in softcopy. It stopped the use of papers in recording transactions, reduced the work of calculators, and allowed automation in preparing financial reports. MS Excel has been improving over the years and is still among the most important accounting software options.

Although accounting has evolved, and we have complex technologies today, Excel is still the primary accounting software for small businesses. The beauty of Excel is that it can be used by anyone with basic computer skills. You can use MS Excel to perform basic accounting tasks such as bookkeeping, invoice management, computations, among others.

MS Excel as an accounting software has several advantages. Although it may be old and less automated as compared to other accounting tools, it has plenty of benefits. Some of its benefits include:

It has the ability to compare datasets. With the Excel accounting software, you can easily compare data sets. For instance, using SUMIFS, you can easily sum up your accounts payable and compare with accounts receivable. Such a simple command will help you determine the overall cash flow position of your business, even without preparing financial reports. With Excel, you can also track your operational costs, determine recurring costs, track your revenue, and other aspects of your cash flow.

One can generate customizable reports. Besides tracking down data sets, you can also use Excel to create reports. You can use your data to create graphs, charts, and tables. The reports created using the software can easily be customized. For example, you may introduce more data points without having to create a new template or open a fresh sheet. The columns and rows in Excel sheets allow you to add columns and rows as you please.

You could automate data entry. One of the biggest problems that accountants have to deal with is having errors in the data. If the accounting data has any errors, you can easily end up compounding the problem throughout your books. You can reduce errors by automating data recording. For instance, you can use a macro to export invoices related data from a CSV file. This way, all the data relating to your invoices will automatically be updated in your Excel sheet to avoid errors.

There are free templates. The beauty of MS Excel is that it comes with ready templates for all financial statements. I have shown you some of the templates in the chapters above. Even if you are not an expert in preparing financial statements, you can easily pull out the necessary template, feed in the necessary data, and use it to generate the necessary report. With Excel, you get free reconciliation sheets, ledgers, invoicing templates, and other finance trackers. Besides the templates that are available for free offline, you can also find online resources by opening a Microsoft account. The online resources will help you set up free accounting templates. You can view YouTube videos that are very helpful in setting up templates, recording data, and computing the data as needed.

QuickBooks

Unlike Excel, which is software that requires plenty of personal input, QuickBooks is a fully automated accounting software. Excel was created for managing different types of datasets and generating reports for all industries. On the contrary, QuickBooks is 100% geared towards bookkeeping and accounting.

In other words, the software is custom made for recording transactions, processing bills, sending invoices, reconciling accounts, and preparing financial reports, among other accounting tasks. Although QuickBooks is one of the best bookkeeping software, it comes at a cost. The free version does not have any of the important accounting features. The pro version will cost you about $299.99 per year, but it is worth the cost.

QuickBooks Pro includes an option for managing your funds. The account allows the user to key in the due dates and all transaction details for recurring invoices. For instance, if you have to pay your employee $4000 at the end of every month, you can allow the software to do payment processing by providing dates that payments are supposed to be released. While invoices are still pending, you can print checks directly from the software. Further, the software documents all transactions for accuracy and transparency.

The reason why QuickBooks is seen as the revolutionary accounting software is that it can actually manage your bank account. If you are using a bank that is accepted, you can link it with the software so that you can easily monitor transactions, check bank balances, read bank statements, and much more from your office.

The other advantage of QuickBooks is that it takes care of expense billing. When carrying out day to day business activities, you may incur expenses such as mileage, dinners, or even large expenses such as prolonged global travel. Such expenses can be summed up and billed to clients later. If you do not have a system of tracking down such expenses, you may end up spending so much money indirectly that later affects your net profits. As the manager or business owner, you have to decide which expenses will be paid for by your business and which ones should be billed to the client. Once you set the boundaries, use your software to track all expenses that are due and report them to your clients.

The other important feature of QuickBooks is the ability to track sales. The software can track sales and instantly generate an invoice. You can program your software to generates sales invoices once certain amounts are attained. For instance, if you normally supply goods to Melisa enterprises and send an invoice once a value of $5,000 is attained, you can use the software to do the same. Allow QuickBooks to track down the sales and send an invoice once the invoicing amount is attained.

The invoices generated can be delivered electronically if you allow your software to automatically send them. However, if you do not want the software to automatically invoice your clients, you may print and send it out manually.

Further, end-users that sign up for Intuit QuickBooks Merchant Services are in a position to accept debit card fees via QuickBooks. They can also scan deposit checks into the software and avoid the long process of having to key in the data.

The other benefit of using QuickBooks is that it can generate some financial reports. Unlike Excel, which requires so much computation to generate any report, QuickBooks can easily generate important reports. You can compare year to year income, expenditure, purchase trends, and even forecast the future. Further, each report can easily be imported into a spreadsheet layout and send electronically to interested parties.

The reason why QuickBooks is one of the popular bookkeeping software is that it is easy to use. Even if you are new to bookkeeping, you can easily understand the interface. The software has a new user setup function, which is easy to follow. The software also provides virtual practice options for new users. Most importantly, most of the functions of the software can be initiated at a click of a button.

Square

Square is one of the popular accounting software for various reasons. Unlike QuickBooks and Excel, Square is more focused on point of sale automation. The software can be used on Android, iOS, and Windows devices. The system has free downloadable software plus a Square magstripe reader. This allows payments to be made via debit and credit cards.

Square is one of the easiest accounting software to use due to the simple drag and drop interface. You can simply set up your point of sale and get running in less than a day. You can drag and drop categories, items, and even customize grids.

Further, Square allows you to manage inventory by changing product properties such as price, name, quality, expiration date, etc. You can also manage access to information, only allowing the right persons to access crucial data. The system uses employee passcodes that can be refreshed every now and then.

The software also makes employee management easy because it provides options for employees to log in at the time of reporting and log out at the time of departure. Most importantly, every transaction is linked to the employee responsible. This way, you reduce the chances of fraud and can easily manage tips and commission.

The software is among the most popular options because it is very simple, direct, and powerful. The software can be downloaded free of charge and provides a simple interface. The fact that it supports drag and drop operations makes it the perfect choice for those with limited technological skills. The software also comes with a ticket management feature which can let you create, save, and add orders with one touch. Since it is easy to use, you can easily integrate it with your daily operations. It will take a shorter time to train your employees as compared to similar programs.

This software makes work easy by automating all the transactions. The use of paper money has been the major cause of fraud in businesses. Thankfully,

Square reduces the chances of money getting lost in the hands of employees. The software also provides cloud storage for digital receipts, invoices, and other source documents. The system can automatically manage inventory and generate sales reports at the end of the trading period.

Square is also useful in generating quick feedback that cannot be attained using other programs. As we have seen, most financial statements can only be prepared quarterly, semi-annually, or annually. In other words, you have to wait for at least 3 months to see how your business is performing. Thankfully, software such as Square can help you figure out valuable analytics in advance. The program can analyze the available sales data on a daily basis and help you observe trends.

Once all the items being traded have been uploaded to the system, it is easy to manage inventory. You can manage your inventory even when you are away from your office. All you have to do is sign in to your dashboard from any device and make changes accordingly. You can also download reports on your current inventory from anywhere in the world.

The other benefit of using Square is that the system can support your marketing efforts. Since the system automates the point of sale services, you can use it to capture customer contact information and send them marketing emails. The software can schedule and automate the sending of marketing messages. The software also allows you to customize birthday offers, emails, and marketing incentives, among others. Using Square, you can create customer profiles, build directory, and send follow up emails whenever necessary.

Besides the point of sale processing, Square easily integrates with other apps. You can integrate Square with Google Sheets, Excel, and other apps to help in managing invoices, inventory, employee payment, and tax processing, among others.

Like any other good app out there, Square developers offer 24-hour support to users. If you find any problems when using the software, you can contact the developers for assistance at any time of the day. They also provide articles, videos, and demos to help you understand the functions of the software.

FreshBooks

Last on our list of the best bookkeeping software is FreshBooks. Although it comes last on this list, it is not in any way inferior to the other programs. It is one of the best and most popular bookkeeping and accounting systems. It is loved due to the fact that it offers plenty of cloud storage. As we have mentioned, one of the major problems that accountants have to handle is data storage. If you store all your data on the cloud, you will not have any problems relating to data loss and security.

FreshBooks helps in collecting, sorting, and tracking transactions. It has proven to be effective in front end accounting, i.e., tracking customer payments, and invoices. Here are some of the key benefits of FreshBooks.

If you do not get your invoices right, you may end up missing some crucial payments. To manage your invoices, you need a system that sets reminders or automates the entire process. FreshBooks is just the perfect software for invoicing. It creates recurring invoices and sends them electronically when it is time for invoicing. The software also allows you to accept payments online and easily customize invoice layouts. FreshBooks system also tracks invoices that have been sent to customers. It can detect the exact time when the invoice is seen and opened. This way, you can avoid cases where clients give excuses for not having seen the invoice.

The other benefit of using FreshBooks is that it helps in tracking time. If you spend a lot of time on a project, you end up reducing its economic viability. The software helps in tracking the time spent on certain projects to avoid cases where too much focus is given to one project.

The benefit of time tracking is that the software helps you determine the billable time. If you end up spending more time on a project than anticipated, you should be able to bill for the extra hours.

The other benefit of FreshBooks is that it has a simple interface. Currently, over 5 million people use paperless billing with FreshBooks. This is because even those who do not have bookkeeping skills can easily use the system. The software does not use complex bookkeeping terms. If you can use a smartphone well, you should not have any problem using FreshBooks in managing payments and invoicing.

Payment integration is a key feature to look at when choosing your accounting software. One of the most integrated accounting software is FreshBooks. For instance, QuickBooks users have to manually create a PayPal account and integrate with the software to process payments. On the contrary, FreshBooks users can automatically integrate their PayPal with the software.

Besides PayPal integration, FreshBooks allows you to pick a third party getaway like Authorize.net to process most online payment options. This means that you can connect to mobile devices and virtual terminal outside FreshBooks.

The other advantage of FreshBooks is that it processes payroll accurately and in time. One of the major problems that owners of small businesses have to face is payroll processing. With FreshBooks, you do not have to be an accountant to process payroll. FreshBooks has an option where employees can enter personal information using a simple mobile app. This way, you do not have to do the job of manually entering employees' information to the database. Once the employees provide the necessary personal information, the app allows you to process your employees' payroll in just a few seconds.

Lastly, FreshBooks is among the most affordable professional bookkeeping software. FreshBooks provides diverse packages that are tailored to different business needs. You will not be forced to pay a huge sum for features you do not need. The payment packages allow you to choose an option that works for your business. Payments start at $19.99 per month, up to $39.95.

Although all the packages share the same features, the numbers of users differ. The basic package allows the software to have up to 5 users at a particular time. The cost increases at a rate of $10 for every extra user per month.

Chapter 6: A Real-world Example Project

Now that we have looked at all the details of accounting, I hope that you are ready to start handling accounting problems at a personal level. To help you gauge your skills after reading this book, I will give you a real-world example. If you are able to complete this task, you should be ready to start managing your accounting books without much trouble. If you are unable to complete the task, do not lose hope, keep practicing with the examples provided throughout the book until you sharpen your skills.

Step 1: Fish Out Financial Statements

Go to Google Finance and choose a company that has recently released financial reports. Bring up the financial data and search through the information. You may also go to the company's website and find the full financials. You will find all the information needed to complete the following challenge.

Step 2: Transfer Financial Information to Excel Spreadsheets

Once you have access to all the financial statements (balance sheets, income statements, and statements of cash flow), transfer the information to an Excel spreadsheet. Use three tabs to represent the information on the three different financial statements.

Step 3: Create Analytical Tools

Once you have the three tabs, create the fourth tab, and label it as ratios. Now go back to our ratios section above and look at the various types of ratios. Calculate all the four types of ratios in the ratios tab. Note down the ratios you get and what they mean.

Step 4: Create and Answer Managerial Questions

After preparing all the necessary ratios, now start interpreting them. To do this, you have to create a fifth tab and label it Analysis. In the 5th tab, note down questions that the manager or an external investor may want to have answered. List about 5 questions and start answering them. For example, "Does this company have enough assets to pay off its current liabilities?" Such questions and answers should help you determine whether your analysis of the data is correct.

Step 5: Find Answers to Your Questions

After writing down all the questions, go back to your ratios tab, and look at the available rations. You should be able to find the answers based on the available data. If you do not find answers, study ratios more to understand what they stand for.

Conclusion

The main goal of the example above is to help you think like an investor. At the end of the day, this book can only be deemed relevant if it helps you solve investor problems. The aim is to ensure that you are in a position to manage basic bookkeeping and accounting tasks. Most investors do not have to go through the hustle of preparing financial reports; however, they must interpret the information provided for them.

Although this book has so much information than you may not be able to understand in one reading, you should at least be able to understand financial reports better. At the end of your reading, you should be able to simplify the data on balance sheets, income statements, and statements of cash flow. You should be in a position to make wise investments based on the financial data provided by your accountant.

If you are done reading the book, and you still feel that there are gaps, you should take a second reading. Go through the book in a slow manner, putting every skill to practice. Start by learning the basics of bookkeeping, such as maintaining the general journal, specialty journals, and the general ledger.

Advance your skills by learning to prepare financial statements. Break down the meaning and contents of each financial statement systematically. This book has explained the information regarding these statements in a simple manner. I have outlined their benefits, uses, and methods of preparation for each statement.

After understanding your financial statements, ensure that you have a close look at accounting rules and analytical tools. You must learn to stay within the prescribed accounting boundaries for all your accounting duties. Further, you must learn to use analytical tools to be able to benefit the most from your financial statements.

Once you are satisfied with your analytical and accounting skills, go ahead and try out the real-life example above. Successfully completing the exercise above will prove that you are ready to start taking care of your accounting tasks.

If this book has benefited you in any way, would you kindly consider leaving a review online where you purchased this book? I appreciate your feedback. Thank you in advance.

www.ingramcontent.com/pod-product-compliance
Lightning Source LLC
Chambersburg PA
CBHW071356210526
45465CB00001B/124